FROM BUS DRIVER TO CEO

FROM BUS DRIVER TO CEO

A PERSONAL JOURNEY TOWARDS BUSINESS OWNERSHIP

Renaldo O. Epps

From Bus Driver to CEO © Renaldo O. Epps, 2020

All rights reserved. This book nor any portion thereof may not be reproduced or used in any manner whatsoever without the expressed written permission the author.

Printed in the U.S. of America
Photo Credit Robert Rodriguez

First Printing, 2020
ISBN 9780578839981

DEDICATION

This book is dedicated to all of the hard-working people in my life who instilled greatness in me:

My mother, Lynda Epps, who taught me that doing the best you can is greatness in and of itself.

My grandmother, Clarice Moore, who used to say, *"Act like a millionaire even if you only have five dollars in your pocket."* These words propelled me forward.

My sister, Valyncea Epps Randall, who teaches that daily love and devotion to family is a must.

And to the host of cousins, nieces, nephews, godchildren and others who have touched my life, I truly want to say *thank you.*

FOREWORD

As an expert on the importance of credit history, the author of *From Bus Driver to CEO* clearly explains not only is it essential for obvious things like qualifying for a loan, or getting a credit card, but also for less obvious things like getting a cellular phone, renting a car or even finding a place to live.

The tips and information in this book are invaluable. Let's face it, at some point in time we have messed up our credit or know someone close to us who has. If that's not you, this is still an important book for you to read as the author sufficiently takes you through the journey of credit repair. When repairing credit, it is crucial to select a company that has specialized in the role. In this case, it is essential to look for a company with experience in accessing the needs and restoring the credit rating. The author also explains that price is another crucial aspect that a business is supposed to use to determine the selection.

This book highlights the need for financing an organization. For most business owners, financial management is a critical issue that affects the success of an organization. Additionally, the conceptual approach of credit management assists a business in understanding employment options, consumer protection, and much more. These are key aspects in enhancing success. Debt is one of the major challenges that business owners encounter. If not effectively controlled, it subjects you to financial pressure. A good credit score is a critical aspect that most financial institutions consider when determining the amount of money a business can access.

The resources in this book are priceless and teach you, if anything else, that believing you can improve your financial life is only half the battle. Yes, it is important to know the why but the how is just as important. Renaldo gives you the "how" on building a better financial life. With the tools and resources in this book, you will find that IT CAN BE DONE!

Mitchell Coles, Paralegal
Notary Public / Notary Signing Agent

TABLE OF CONTENTS

Dedication	5
Foreword	7
Introduction	11

FUNDING YOUR BUSINESS

Introduction	19
Good Credit Bad Credit	23
Credit Repair	33
Debt Management	57
Financial Literacy	69
Land Banking	75
Saving Tools	79
Leaving Your Nine-to-Five	83

PROTECTING YOUR BUSINESS

Introduction	89
Types of Insurance	91
Business Insurance	95
Casualty & Property Insurance	103
Health Insurance	117
Legal Protection	125
Life Insurance	129
Travel Insurance	139
Identity Insurance	145

GROWING YOUR BUSINESS

Introduction	155
Home Based Business	157
Technical Options	167
Education vs Experience	173
Legalizing Your Business	181

A CALL TO ACTION

Change Your Mindset	191
About the Author	193

INTRODUCTION

I have always loved money. I was taught, *"Even if you only have five dollars in your pocket, act like you're a millionaire!"* When I was a teenager I had two jobs. I worked at McDonalds and Phil-a-job (a city of Philadelphia program to keep kids off the street). I remained at McDonald's until my short stint in the U.S. Army. I wasn't used to all the screaming and yelling, but while in the service, I met some great people and learned many lifelong lessons.

In my early twenties the search for self began. I was also seeking acceptance. My first step was to grasp the concept of wanting more. I started college with the help of an African American welfare social worker. I was in his office about to transfer my benefits from my mother to myself when he asked me about my hopes and dreams and told me that a scholarship to a local community college was available if I wanted it. I graduated as a paralegal and my love for education was born. Then I got a job as a police officer at a military base in Philadelphia. That's where my love for the law was born.

I eventually began working for a local transportation company, enrolled in college, and graduated with a doctorate in religious sciences – only to find myself unemployable. When I was in my thirties, I moved to Wilmington, DE. HIV/AIDS was running rampant in the city. I wanted to give back to African American men in the gay community, so I joined a support group for African American gay men. Little did I know being in that group was an interview. A local HIV/AIDS organization was searching for a "black gay guy" to be the face of their new funding program.

I began working part-time as a consultant and my job was to provide gay clubs and barbershops with condoms. I noticed that the "white clients" got more services that the blacks and I became angry. It was my belief that people were making money off of the backs of marginalized people. After that I was asked to leave.

After being terminated from that position, a powerful African American woman approached me with an offer to lead the educational department of her organization. Her company focused on educating high risk youth on the dangers of unprotected sex and drug use. This was my first professional job title as Ed.D. During this time, I continued pursuing my educational endeavors. I received two addition degrees: M.Div. and Ph.D.

When I hit thirteen years of service with the bus company, I started thinking about the future and retirement. I began saving 30% of my take home pay. As I looked for the opportunity to make more income, I had the idea to start my own business.

It all began with a phone call. One day I was sitting home answering ads about working from home. I received a phone call from a man named Mr. Chamblee who suggested I think about business ownership. I had no idea that owning my own business would be the best thing for me. I was scheduled to meet him the following Saturday and attend a presentation on marketing and networking. *"Oh boy,"* I thought, *"not one of those events again."* When I got in the car, I voiced my disdain. He asked me to keep an open mind. After the presentation, I was hooked! I understood how money worked and began to think seriously about business ownership. I was very interested in the tax advantages of small business ownership.

The biggest issue for me was time. I was back in school yet again and I was still working full time as a bus driver. I had too many years of experience (and was making too much money) to quit. Shortly after that, on July 31st, **Dr. Renaldo Epps Consulting Group LLC** was born. July 31st is a special date in my life. It is the same date that I began working for the bus company.

Back when I was working for the at-risk youth group, I noticed a divide between the digital world and the services that providers needed. I purchased a franchise to jumpstart my business ownership journey, and then decided to take on the immense challenge of attending law school. As a full-time law student, I am learning first-hand the intricacies of contracts, business formations, and customer awareness. While is it challenging, and leaves hardly any free time, I am blessed to have the energy to accomplish what few have done.

While building my business, I noticed another gap in services. Once again, I went out and purchased another franchise, repeated what I did with the first one, and it became even more successful. The next component of my organization was a hands-on services provider. I contracted with a well-known fortune 500 company to provide supervisory and analytical retrieval. The final step was to incorporate in a safe state for businesses, which happens to be the state I reside in – Delaware.

Since then I have expanded to New York City, Washington, D.C., and opened a satellite office in Atlanta, GA. My company reached a milestone in 2019 when due to a split, **Dr. Renaldo Epps Consulting Group LLC** birthed **24-7 Digital Solutions LLC** to handle my online customers and the digital components of the business.

Dr. Renaldo Epps Consulting Group LLC continues to operate marketing services.

My philosophy is *"Lead by example with the highest ethical standards."* Welcome to my world! I hope you enjoy the read.

This book is written for all the Black and Brown African American men who look like me who struggle with taking their rightful places of leadership within the community.

Let's not struggle anymore.

Funding Your Business

INTRODUCTION

Raising Money for Your Business

When I started my business raising money was tight. I had a plan for every penny that came in. I knew months in advance where my money was coming from and where it was going.

Knowing your cash flow can help alleviate financial heartaches. I used my nine-to-five job to fund my dream. I worked extra hours to make extra money. I used household items to create a workspace: an old table to make a desk; an old place mat for a desk blotter. I probably "borrowed" every ink pen I could find to build my stash of office supplies. Many nights I fell asleep sitting straight up my chair – a very hard chair I might add. I wouldn't change that experience for the world. I had fun doing it and that was important to me.

Is it a Business or a Hobby?

First you have to ask yourself whether you are operating a business or a hobby. Many people start hobbies that make a little money. Let me give you an example. Let's say someone's Grandmother only bakes cakes to sell around the holidays. That's a hobby. But if your friend sells cupcakes all year long, that may become a business.

The definition of a business is the practice of making one's living by engaging in commerce (buying and selling). Legitimate businesses operate legally.

You can use your job to help fund your business. If there is a way for you to work overtime once a week, that may create extra income for you to put towards your business. Taking on a part-time job can also help you find additional dollars to put towards your business.

You can always go the route of services such as ride sharing companies and package delivering services (using your own vehicle) to generate streams of income for your business. If done correctly - you have the proper licensing - you can grow a healthy fund to run a viable business.

Use what you already have before purchasing new items. Many people run out and buy all the stuff they think they need to open and operate a business and never use any of it. I have a rule in my business that was taught by my grandmother: *only buy it once*. For example, if I purchase a new laptop then I plan on using it until it needs to be replaced – regardless of how many years and how many advertisements there are to upgrade to a newer model.

The Credit Card Dilemma

I am not a fan of using credit cards to grow a business unless you have a way to pay the bill in full once it arrives. You will need your credit cards to fund your licenses online, so my advice would be to only use them sparingly.

For anything else, only use them for your most needed purchases. Ask yourself, "Can I write this off for my business?" "Do I really need to make this purchase right now?" If the answer to both questions is "Yes" then look for the item at a reasonable price and go ahead and make the purchase with a credit card. I try to purchase items that have a bonus attached to them.

The SBA (Small Business Association)

The SBA is a government agency established to provide assistance to small businesses. One of the main functions of the SBA is to provide counseling and aid to individuals trying to start and grow a business.

They offer help free of charge with planning. They also sponsor local events that can help you build business connections in your community.

What does your business plan say about financing and funding? Yes, the dreaded business plan. Most people hate this part, but I consider the business plan to be the road map to your success. Mapping out your next move can help you know where and how your money should be spent.

SBA's offer a variety of loan programs for very specific purposes. Small business loans can be a life saver but don't look at them in the beginning. Your business needs to generate money before you go down that "rabbit hole."

GOOD CREDIT BAD CREDIT

WHY SHOULD I HAVE GOOD CREDIT?

Having good credit can be beneficial for you in many ways. Day by day, people are becoming more and more dependent on credit to make decisions about their life – from what they should purchase to whether or not to make a purchase at all.

Nowadays, good credit is used as a gateway to all types of benefits. Many institutions have established that a good credit history is the number one qualifier before they extend any services to you.

Insurance

Insurance corporations use your credit rating to determine which insurance package to recommend. Through your credit, they decide what rate to offer you for auto, life, and homeowner's insurance. Like most lending companies, in their eyes, the higher your credit rating, the better your reliability.

Employment Options

Most employers also run credit checks on prospective new hires, and more times than not, all things being equal, the person with good credit stands a better chance of getting hired. Why? Because an individual with a good credit report is considered to be more trustworthy. That type of person has a proven track record of keeping their word – at least when it comes to paying their bills.

Consumer Protection

Cash purchases are almost always better than debit or credit purchases because of issues with interest. It also helps you better budget your money. Cash only purchases don't come with a zero-fraud liability guarantee but having good credit (and using it) gives you better consumer protection through warranties and fraud protection on some purchases.

Rental Options

A good credit rating expands your renting options. As stated earlier, a good credit history reveals your reliability. It is a fact that rental agencies lean more towards credit worthy people. Even if you're renting from a private owner and you intend to pay your rent in cash (or check/money order) before you sign your lease and are handed your keys, that property owner will most likely run a quick credit check on you.

Conclusion

As you can see, there is a world of advantages when you have good credit rating, including better employment opportunities, job success, lower interest rates, consumer protection, and better housing options.

You can turn a negative credit history into a positive one and instantly improve your quality of life.

THE SIDE EFFECTS OF BAD CREDIT

If your credit cards are all maxed out and your bills are overdue, your credit history has already been negatively affected.

The higher your level of debt – including credit card debt – the greater your credit score will be impacted. If you don't catch up in a timely fashion, your credit score is sure to plummet.

If you're wondering what the big deal is about a low credit score, the answer boils down to the fact that no matter where turn, you won't be able to avoid being judged based your credit score. Having bad credit can make life extremely difficultly, from finding a place to live to finding a job.

Listed below are some of the most common problems you might face because of bad credit:

- Money lenders view an applicant with bad credit as a higher risk than an applicant with good credit. Over time you might end up paying more in interest to lenders because of the risk they take by lending money to people with bad credit score.
- Some lenders and creditors will think that your bad credit rating is so risky that they will reject your application all together.
- Did you know that landlords check your credit before approving you for an apartment? The sad truth is that having bad credit can very well leave you homeless.
- Sometimes utility companies will run a credit check on you as part of their application process. If you have a bad credit rating, you might end up paying an extremely high security deposit to have a utility in your name.

- Cell phone companies check your credit as well. They are extending a month of service to you, so they need to know how reliable your payments will be. If you have bad credit, you may have to get a prepaid cell phone with a month-to-month contract, which in some cases is much more expensive.
- There are certain jobs, especially in the finance industry, that require you to have a good credit history. You could be turned down for a job because of bad credit, a bankruptcy, high debt, or outstanding bills.
- According to insurance companies, people with low credit scores have a higher percentage of claims filed than those with good credit. Because of this, insurance companies charge higher premiums to those with low credit scores.
- Starting a new business might require a business loan. A bad credit rating could limit the amount of funds you will be able to borrow for a new business, even if you have the greatest idea with all the necessary data and documents to prove its viability, necessity, and success.
- Good credit is necessary for any loan you may apply for. For example, if you want a car loan, you might get denied because of bad credit. Or, if you do get approved, it will be with an extremely high interest rate.
- Numerous calls from debt collectors are another annoying side effect of a poor credit rating.

FIVE HELPFUL HINTS TO INCREASE YOUR CREDIT SCORE

According to the National Foundation for Credit Counselling, more people are embarrassed to admit their credit scores (30%) than their weight (12%). If you are one of these people, there are a few steps you can take to increase your credit score in as little as 60 days!

Don't be afraid of that 450 anymore! With these 5 *credit score hints*, your credit score will skyrocket, seeing you hit 700 and above.

The first thing to do before you start is to get your hands on a copy of your credit report through annualcreditreport.com.

Once you know what you're working with, set yourself a goal to jump 50 points (or however much you feel is reasonable) in 3-4 months and immediately put some of these steps into practice.

1. Fight errors

One of the easiest ways to increase your credit score is to fight any errors that may be on your credit report. Mistakes do happen and they can cost you quite a few points, so fix these issues as quickly as possible.

2. Talk to your creditors about existing overdue balances

You can't hide your missed payments under a rug like dust around the house, so be up front and try to make a deal with your creditors to erase the debt. Send a letter asking that they attach a 'Paid as Agreed' status on your account in exchange for you paying the remainder of the bill.

This is a sure-fire way to increase your credit score. Just make sure they agree in writing so there are no disputes down the road.

3. Get a credit card

Having a credit card or two can do wonders to increase your credit score. As long as you pay your bills on time and don't overspend or hit you credit limit too often, you will see a nice jump in your credit score.

If you already have a credit card, make sure you are aware of your credit limit. Contact the issuer regularly to check your limit. If a drop has occurred in your limit, you may be maxing out the card without even realizing it, which will penalize you further.

4. Minimize credit card use

Don't use your credit card for everything. By keeping your usage below 30% (even less if possible) you could increase your credit score by showing that you can use credit effectively without being too dependent on it.

5. Pay your bills before they're due

This is a big one that catches a lot of people unaware. Another good way to increase your credit score is to pay your bills on time. That accounts for 35% of your total credit score! If you constantly forget to pay on time, use the automatic payment option.

Conclusion

The hints listed here will help you improve your credit rating and help you overcome a poor credit score in quick and easy ways. Stay in contact with your creditors, don't overuse your credit card and pay your bills on time. Do these things and you will increase your credit score quicker than you can imagine.

FLUCTUATING CREDIT

Does your credit card balances change from month to month? Is the amount of available credit on your cards frequently changing? Then you may have a fluctuating credit score. These are just some of the factors which can affect your credit score. Once you have examined these factors closely, you will find areas for improvement. Below are some factors to consider.

Did you max out on any credit card?

Sometimes there are emergency purchases like unforeseen medical bills or sudden home and car repairs. Even if you are not in the position of paying off the balance in full, you should consider paying as much as you can each month and stay current with your payments. This way you can keep your payment history solid and avoid getting too close to your credit limit. It is recommended to keep your card balances at or below one third of their limit.

Have you applied for new credit recently?

Did you apply for an auto loan, a mortgage or a new credit card? When you venture into the market for a home or car loan, your credit will show additional inquiries. You should remember that hard inquiries stay on your credit report for up to two years, but soft credit inquires don't affect your score at all.

Is there any suspicious information listed in your report?

If there is any suspicious information on your credit report, you should notify all three credit reporting agencies right way. Suspicious information could be a red flag that your identity has been stolen. If your card is suddenly maxed out or if new credit cards are suddenly opened in your name, that could lower your credit score.

Did you make any late payments?

It may be time to adapt a new approach to paying your bills on time. You should consider paying bills promptly not only a responsibility, but an accomplishment. Consider the automatic online bill payment option. Some creditors will also let you set up payment reminders via your account.

Do you ever contact your creditors?

If you are not paid up to date on all of your accounts, a creditor is probably the last person you want to talk to. On the other hand, reaching out to your credit card companies directly can help you resolve issues. Before contacting them, check with your financial advisor to make sure there aren't other solutions that would be better for your financial situation. After all, negotiating your credit card debt can also have aa negative impact to your credit score.

HOW TO MAINTAIN A GOOD CREDIT REPORT

Do you know how a creditor decides whether or not to approve your credit card application? By reviewing the information contained in your credit report. Namely, your identity, your existing credit information, your public records and any recent inquiries on your credit profile.

Tips to maintain a good credit report:

- Using a credit card to buy things you otherwise cannot afford is a big mistake. You can avoid credit card debt when you purchase only what you can afford to pay for. If you cannot afford to pay for it in cash, you cannot afford to charge it.
- Most people end up with credit card debt because they do not have the cash to afford emergencies like a sudden illness or major car and home repairs, so they are forced to charge the expenses to a credit card. However, having an emergency fund would allow you to use the cash you have saved when emergencies occur and help you avoid this type of debt.
- It is also a good idea to avoid balance transfers from one credit card to another, unless it is to take advantage of a lower interest rate. Otherwise, the transfer fees will increase your balance. Keeping balance transfers to minimum will help you avoid debt.
- Paying off your credit card balances in full each month is another good technique. If you want to avoid credit card debt altogether, you should pay off your credit card balances every month. This way you will not have to worry about meeting the minimum monthly payments, or exceeding your limit, because you won't have a balance. This will also improve your credit score.

- One of the worst ways to use your credit card is for cash advances. If you are using your credit card to get cash, there is something wrong with your finances. A cash advance is one of the first signs of credit card debt. You need to work on fixing your budget and creating an emergency fund so that you won't have to use cash advances in an emergency.
- It is advised to read through each credit card agreement to make sure you understand how the interest rates are applied to your accounts, when late fees are charged, and whether or not your interest rates will increase. These issues should be clearly understood so that you can avoid credit card debt.
- There is no point in keeping multiple credit cards, because the more cards you have, the more cards you will use. Usually, one or two credit cards is enough. Even if you have self-control, it is better not to be tempted by thousands of dollars in available credit. If you don't want to cut down on the number of cards you have, then at least cut down the number of cards you keep in your wallet. This can also help you avoid credit card debt.

CREDIT REPAIR

WHAT IS A CREDIT REPAIR COMPANY?

The importance of your credit score should never be underestimated. Even people with favorable credit scores sometimes have a hard time obtaining bank loans and low interest credit card accounts. A poor credit history can be a nightmare to many people, especially those who are thinking of applying for a car loan or deciding on financing options for a new house. Your credit history speaks volumes about who you are, especially how responsible you are with keeping your word and meeting your obligations. If your credit history is unfavorable, you need to do something about it.

But there is still hope for you. Rather than succumb to the pain of the situation, it is recommended that you look for companies that specialize in credit repair. The abundance of available companies that specialize in credit repair is promising for you in terms of the many options you have for improving your image with lenders.

Credit repair professionals solve your issues with bad credit by locating miscalculations on your credit report. Moreover, they counsel you on how you can improve your bad credit score by finding errors on your credit report. They advise you on how to can clean your credit and keep it from reflecting any late payments, recoveries, conclusions, or compilations. But if you think this can be done overnight, you are mistaken. This is not a one-step procedure, but by developing self-discipline and applying good saving habits you can repair your credit.

CHECKLIST TO FINDING A CREDIT REPAIR COMPANY

Is the agency accredited?

The first thing you should consider before moving forward with any credit counseling agency is accreditation. Although most companies are non-profit, you shouldn't just select the first agency you run across. You should always do a little research. A leading source for accreditation is the Council on Accreditation.

How will they help you?

A credit counselor can provide lots of information and advice about how to help you regain control of your finances and how to help you establish a budget. This advice should be free but if your situation warrants it, they may suggest a paid service called a DMP (Debt Management Plan).

Will their services have any effect on your credit score?

Taking advice from a credit counseling agency or entering into a DMP will not damage your credit score. There are some creditors who may be concerned if they see this on your credit history – and it will certainly show up. But if you're paying bills late, this probably isn't your greatest concern.

What are the fees?

Advice should always be free, but when you enroll in a DMP you have to pay a monthly fee. Most times the fee won't be more than fifty dollars and is sometimes waived for those who are unable to afford it. However, when an agency tries to direct you to a DMP without going over the details of your credit history – consider that a bad sign. There is a reason this is called credit *counseling*. They should counsel you first before attempting to sell you any services.

Do they offer any additional resources?

Some agencies offer personal finance courses that cover budgeting, saving, and bill management. Normally those services do not come with a price tag.

What is their privacy policy?

The confidentiality of your personal information should be of utmost importance to your credit counselor. You should make sure the credit agency has a privacy policy before doing business with them. They should send you a contract and give you ample time to review before you sign and return it.

How do they promote themselves?

A good non-profit credit counselling agency normally has a huge advertising budget on every platform, including digital, print, and billboards.

IN CLOSING

The most common mistake consumers make is waiting too long to get help. If you have a debt problem, you fall under the norm more than most, so don't let embarrassment stop you from seeking help.

WHAT TO LOOK FOR IN A CREDIT REPAIR SERVICE

Features

You should look for credit repair companies that are reputable and on par with industry standards such as: being licensed, having a refund policy, providing privacy protection, and offering special discounts.

Services

A personal account manager, no-cost meetings, and terms and conditions that are clear, understandable, and followed.

Help and Support

Help and support is one of the basic services that good credit repair companies provide. Representatives should respond to emails within 24 business hours and properly answer each inquiry.

Ease of Use

A good and reputable credit repair company is also user-friendly. While searching, you must look at the company's account management system. They should provide online interactions in a smooth and effective way. If they have a user-friendly network, you will easily find all pertinent information and you'll be able to navigate through their online process with little to no issues.

Experience

This is one of the most important things to consider as you look for a credit repair company. While you will be confronted with a variety of choices, this does not mean that every company will meet your needs.

Two companies may be in the same area so experience is sometimes the only thing that will give an edge over the other. Sometimes the best thing to do is to work with the company that has been providing repair services for the longest amount of time. This usually means that they have already been tried and tested in the marketplace, so they have the expertise to tackle your needs and restore your credit rating to good standing.

Research

Another important thing you can do is to seek recommendations from others, especially those you know personally. You can also go online and read reviews that have been shared by people who have already used the services of various credit repair companies in the past. Sometimes, through their experiences alone, you will be able to weigh the pros and cons of the services each company provides and separate the more favorable companies from the less favorable ones, based on your specific needs.

Price

The fact that you are looking for credit repair services means that you are or have been in a bad financial season. Working with companies that promise to repair your credit score will almost always results in additional costs on your part. Sometimes your first or second choice is considerably more expensive than others. Because of this, it is imperative that you consider the rates as well as the services of each company.

Choice

The last step is to narrow the list of the companies you researched down to two or three companies that are the best of the best. All that's left at that point is to make your selection. At the end of the day, you've done your due diligence because you exhausted all possible means to determine which credit repair company is the best for you.

Licensed to Operate

Another important factor to consider is whether or not the credit repair company is licensed to operate. Look for permits that are granted by the government and other relevant agencies. That will prove the legitimacy of the credit repair company. More often than not, such documents will be displayed in their offices (or on their website) as a way of legitimizing of their reputation. If you work with an unlicensed company, you run the risk of being scammed rather than being given a helping hand.

Reviews & Recommendations

Reading reviews written by people who have used a particular credit repair company can be found online. This is an excellent way for you to objectively weigh each company's pros and cons. Alternatively, if you do not trust the opinions that are given by strangers, you can ask people you know personally for their recommendations.

A good credit repair company has a favorable reputation. Another way to verify this is to look up any possible issues or complaints with the Better Business Bureau. This will assure you of the best possible outcome and the best value for your money.

Physical Office vs Online Services

It's also a good idea to verify if the credit repair company has an actual physical office address or if the company only exists online. If the company only exists online, all of your transactions will be electronic, and you lose the trust that face-to-face interactions bring. Therefore, it may be more beneficial to do business with credit repair companies that you are able to visit in person.

Conclusion

As you can see, looking for the best credit repair company can prove to be a tedious task. Nonetheless, following the steps below will make it easier for you to find the best company for you.

- Pay your bills on time. If you have a tendency to forget or if you are busy, use reminders or pay online.
- Read your credit report regularly and carefully, make sure all activity listed was done by you or under your direct supervision.
- Immediately report any errors you spot and get them corrected.
- Keep your personal information safe. Be cautious of online fraud and identity theft.
- Do not apply for a new credit card unless you really need one.
- Reducing excessive use of your credit cards can also be helpful.
- Remember to monitor your credit score.

Repairing your credit score is a slow and tedious process. It can take time, so you must have patience.

WHEN TO START REPAIRING YOUR CREDIT?

When is the right time to start repairing you credit score? You don't know what your credit rating is, but you're sure it's not as good as it should be. Below are some signs that indicate you may need to repair your credit.

- When you have been denied a credit card, that may be a sign that you need credit repair. Credit card companies always send you an adverse action notice which includes specific reasons why your credit card application was denied. If you were denied credit because of information in your credit report, then you are entitled to a free copy of the report.
- When your utilities are in someone else's name. Utility services will run a credit check before deciding whether to extend their services to you. If you are unable to get electricity - or any other utility - in your name, it is time for you to check your credit report, find out what negative items are affecting your score, and fix your credit.
- When debt collectors start calling you on a regularly basis, it means creditors have turned your accounts over to a collection agency. Collection accounts also appear on your credit report and can affect your ability to get approved for loans and credit cards. Credit repair will involve paying off these collection accounts or disputing them if they don't belong on your report.
- When you need someone to co-sign on a loan because you are not able to get approved on your own, it means you need credit repair. Once your credit has been restored, you'll be able to get a loan without someone signing for you.

Other situations to consider:

- Is your credit rating keeping you from getting a job? Many employers include credit checks in their decision-making process for new hires and promotions. This is especially true for top financial executive positions. Putting off repairing your credit could be keeping you from that dream job you always wanted.
- Landlords also check credit. A poor credit score can also cause your rental application to be denied. There are some landlords who are lenient with one or two late payments, but they take major delinquencies very seriously. To save yourself the embarrassment of being denied for an apartment, it is a good idea to begin the process of cleaning up your credit report now.
- Credit card companies have been known to raise interest rates as a result of information obtained on your credit report. If you have a history of late payments with other creditors or if a new collection account appears on your credit report, your interest rates could increase. This is yet another reason not to put off repairing your credit.

CLEANING YOUR CREDIT

Cleaning, repairing and rebuilding your credit can be very tedious. The steps to cleaning your credit depend on exactly what's on your report.

Before you begin the process of cleaning your credit, you should order a copy of your report and review each item for any negative explanations. This will give you an idea of what you need to do to improve your credit score.

Below are some of the most common credit report problems and some tips to fix them:

Incorrect Information

To date, the easiest thing to fix on your credit report is inaccurate information. Don't overlook minor clerical errors, because they can definitely damage your credit score. You should immediately submit a dispute to have any inaccurate information removed.

Past Due Accounts

Your payment history has the largest impact on your credit score. Late payments, charge-offs, and accounts in collection hurt your credit score more than anything else. If you have accounts that are 30 or 60 days late, getting current will keep them from taking a toll on your credit score. Once accounts are 90-days in arrears, they are considered extremely delinquent. Try negotiating with debt collectors and creditors to remove collection accounts and charge-offs from your report.

Over Limit Credit Card Balances

The level of debt you have is the second largest impact on your credit score. Ideally, the balance of each credit card should be at or below 30% of its limit. The first step should be to focus on bringing your credit card balances below their limit. Once that task is complete, the next step is to bring all of your credit card balances below the 30% level.

Judgments

Civil judgments include cases where a collection agency, credit card company, or lender, takes you to court over unpaid debts. These types of outstanding judgments should be paid as soon as possible, because otherwise they will negatively your credit until they're paid off or they fall off after seven years - whichever comes first.

Student Loan Defaults

Defaults are not always permanent. You can talk with your lender to find out what your options will bring your student loan out of default. Almost always you have to make several months of timely payments before your loan will be considered current again.

Tax Liens, Foreclosures, and Bankruptcies

These types of entries do not require any repair unless the entry is inaccurate. In that case you would use the dispute process to have that item removed from your credit report. You might have to work with banks and courts to have your records updated. If a serious delinquency, like a bankruptcy, is listed on your credit report, focus on rebuilding your credit by adding positive payments to your credit history.

THE CREDIT REPAIR CLOUD

Did you know that there is a software program that can assist you in repairing your credit? It's called a "Cloud-Based CRMS" (Customer Relationship Management System). Cloud-based simply means that all data is stored, managed, and processed on a network of remote servers hosted on the internet, rather than through on-site local servers or desktop computers in brick-and-mortar businesses. For example, if you have ever opened and used an email account, technically you have already used cloud-based software.

Business owners who use cloud-based software find that it is a relatively simple way to start, run and grow a lucrative Credit Repair Business. The system emails the business owner their schedule every morning; it manages their clients; and it captures leads from their website, team members and affiliates. This software is a convenient personal assistant who never takes time off.

Security

Most major software companies are moving to cloud-based systems. It is a better, more efficient way to work, because cloud servers are always consistent and always super-fast. You don't have to worry about the technical side of things because all backups, upgrades, security, and uptime issues are managed by the software company. Cloud-based software systems are very safe. With traditional software, employees save data on their laptops and other portable devices. Laptops can be stolen, computers are rarely backed up properly, and are sometimes not updated with proper security patches. With a Credit Repair Cloud System, your data is stored with bank-level security encryption and backed-up daily in a highly secured data center.

Client Portals

Cloud-based credit repair services also come equipped with client portals where you can login, sign agreements, choose items to dispute on your credit report, and monitor your status every step of the way.

Cloud-based software can be used by anyone with a web browser. You don't have to download any programs or worry about any upgrades. There is no need to install any equipment, and you can access the cloud from any device with internet service.

Client portals also:

- Imports your credit report very quickly.
- Analyses negative items, saving you hours of typing.
- Pulls data from a credit report and creates a perfect dispute letter in seconds.
- Helps you keep your bookkeeping records organized.
- Send out professional invoices for you.

CREDIT REPAIR LOANS

If you need to build or rebuild your credit, a loan can help. Taking out a loan should always be your last option, but it can be useful if you plan carefully and manage your funds thoughtfully.

The credit repair loan process is simple. There are certain options provided by the loan companies. You start by selecting the amount you wish to save. Those funds are secured for you in a special savings account. You might have an agreement to pay the loan back over a 12-month term and you have to be sure to make your payments on time. Your monthly payments will create a positive payment history, which is reported to the major credit bureaus.

When you have repaid the loan in full, you will have access to the funds which were on hold for you in the designated savings account. This type of loan can help you repair and re-establish your credit. If you're careful, you can also begin to save, and even put a down payment on a vehicle or some other major expense.

When you get a credit repair loan, the amount you receive is be used to pay off all of your creditors simultaneously. After your debtors are paid, the money you owe can be paid off according to the monthly installments by the loan company. This type of loan is only meant for people who want to repair their credit.

Credit repair loans are secured with lower interest rates than the interest rate of most loans. The interest rates are not as low as it is for people with good or excellent credit, but it's not as high as what other credit-marred borrowers are forced to pay, either.

Since your loan will be secured by a credit repair agency, your credit history most likely will not considered in the approval process. If you decide to cancel the loan or if you become delinquent, the company can close the loan and return the principal payments you made back to you. This should be done the day before the loan is considered 30 days delinquent, so there would be no negative payment history to be reported.

BANKRUPTCY AND CREDIT REPAIR

Improving your credit after a bankruptcy, foreclosure, or short sale can be difficult, but it is not impossible. It's important to know what effect each of these events will have on your credit.

With bankruptcies, the hit to your credit score depends on how good your credit was before the bankruptcy. If it was good, your score will take a bigger hit than if your credit was already in the dumps.

After a foreclosure, your eligibility to obtain new credit will depend on the reason you lost your home. If the loss was due to a recent economic recession, and not because of poor financial habits, you may be able to obtain another mortgage sooner rather than later.

Steps you can take for credit repair when it comes to a bankruptcy:

After you file bankruptcy, you will receive multiple credit card offers. Having a past bankruptcy doesn't mean you will never have another credit card again. Getting one or two credit cards after you file could actually help you rebuild your credit. Whether you should get a new credit card or not actually depends on your ability to repay the debt and your ability to use the card responsibly.

The main reason to obtain a post-bankruptcy credit card is to start rebuilding your credit. Most of the time your credit will take a hit as soon as you file. An easy way counter that is to apply for a new card, use it for small purchases, and pay the bill on time every month. As usual, the credit card company will report your payment history to the credit reporting agency, which will increase your credit score over time.

Most people who file bankruptcy do so because they do not have money to pay off their debts. Once you have obtained bankruptcy discharge, you are no longer responsible for the debt you had prior to filing for bankruptcy. This makes you a viable option for any credit card company.

But don't forget the budget you prepared for your bankruptcy case. Make sure that you really do have the income for new credit card payments. If not, you should wait for your circumstances to get better. Create a budget and stick to it, especially after a bankruptcy. If you filed bankruptcy because of credit card debt, just ask yourself honestly whether you will be able to keep yourself from using the card just because you have it.

The bottom line is that getting a new line of credit after bankruptcy will only help you repair your credit if you are responsible. If you cannot afford the payments because you still don't have sound financial judgment, it is better to hold off until you know you can handle it.

CREDIT REPAIR AFTER A DIVORCE

After a divorce, you may have to rebuild or repair your credit. It might be difficult, especially with everything else you may be dealing with, but in most cases it is definitely necessary.

A better credit score will not happen overnight, but every good decision will move you one step closer. If you have a steady income after your divorce, begin by living on a budget. Repairing and rebuilding your credit is first and foremost about paying your bills on time. And for that, you need to have steady income. Child support and alimony qualify, but if that is your only source of income, hopefully it is high enough to meet all your monthly expenses.

Whatever your source of income is, you should manage it well. A budget can help you if you are not used to managing money. If your ex-spouse always took care of the bills, then it may take some time for you to get used to paying bills and following a budget.

First, you need to check your credit report and credit score to see where you stand. Just pull a recent copy of your report, it has all information you need. Also, make sure that any joint debts with your ex-spouse are completely paid off. You will never have complete control of your credit history if you still have open accounts with your ex-spouse. Their credit will continue to affect yours even after your divorce is final.

The only bills you are responsible for are the ones in your name only, and the same goes for your spouse. Balance transfers, refinanced loans, and bill consolidations are options that both of you can use to restructure your debt individually, in your own names.

However, if you have any joint debt should try your best to stay on top of the payment history for the sake of your individual credit. Any missed payments can still affect your credit score even if the judge declared your spouse responsible for those bills. All joint credit cards should be canceled to prevent future charges from being made on the account.

You need to figure out how to get a handle on the bills you cannot afford to pay. It is common for ex-spouses to struggle financially in the months and even years before and after a divorce. If you're having trouble paying your bills, you can seek help through a consumer credit counseling company. The counselor might be able to help you assess your financial situation and decide the best way forward. The credit counseling agency may suggest that you file bankruptcy, depending on the severity of your situation.

For women who are planning to go back to their maiden name after a divorce, it's good idea to make sure the name change is done legally before attempting to re-establish your credit. This way, your new account will be issued in the legal name you will use going forward. It is advised to contact your existing creditors and have them change the name on all your old accounts as well.

CREDIT REPAIR SCAMS

While many credit repair companies do a great job in helping people with bad credit, a number of fraudulent credit repair company scams have also been in operation. Scam cases have been reported for some time now and if you are looking for a credit repair provider it would be prudent to keep the following tips in mind in order to find a legitimate company that knows exactly what they're doing.

Always trust your instincts

Although this point does not directly relate to the work done by any credit repair company, it is important to note that your instincts are usually right. If you feel that an agency or company you're considering is not good enough, it is better to move on. Instincts also go a long way in prompting you to do a more thorough background check on a company before working with them in the future.

Do a thorough background check

It is also important to do a comprehensive background check on the credit repair company you are considering working with. In your check, look for the registration status of the company and whether or not the location is a physical address or a mailing address. Any information that doesn't look right should be a red flag for you to pull out of any agreements you may have begun.

Go with established providers

Finding a credit repair company is easy, but in case you feel that you don't have time to do a comprehensive background check, going with an established provider will save you the trouble. Established providers are ideal because at least with them you know you are working with an experienced company that is likely to have mastered (and perfected) industry standards.

Read customer reviews and testimonials

You can find reviews and testimonials online about many credit repair companies in most search engines. Before you choose any company it is important to read through as many comments as you can from former customers and clients. This will give you a better perspective on how to choose the right company for you.

Requesting money up-front

You will know that you have encountered a fraudulent credit repair company if the company insists that you pay them upfront. It would be good for you if you stay away from companies that make such demands.

Ads that promise a "New Credit Identity"

Any company that promises you a "new credit identity" is unscrupulous. Any company that says they can help you hide bad credit history for a fee is not to be trusted. If you agree and pay them, they will provide you with an Employer Identification Number (EIN). This number is used by businesses to report financial information to the IRS and Social Security Administration. It cannot be used as a substitute for your Social Security Number (which is connected to your bad credit history).

These companies might tell you that this process is legal, but that is not true. Some companies have been known to sell stolen Social Security numbers, often belonging to children. Doing so means you would then be involved in identity theft which will only result in legal troubles. It is a federal crime to lie on a credit or loan application, or to misrepresent your Social Security Number.

LEGALLY REPAIRING YOUR CREDIT

According to some statistics, 79% of all credit reports contain some type of errors. These errors can cause serious harm to your credit rating and can even cost you thousands of dollars due to extremely high interest fees on mortgages, car loans, and other forms of credit. These errors can also prevent you from owning your own home, getting a new car, or even getting a good credit card with reward offers.

Unfortunately, a large majority of people do not realize that they can easily and legally fix their credit rating by contacting the credit bureaus directly. You also have the option of using a legal credit repair company to assist you. Appointing an experienced credit repair attorney is another great idea.

There are a lot of credit repair companies that use unscrupulous and dishonest methods of credit repair. Such companies are guilty of not adhering to the Credit Repair Organizations Act (CROA) which is a federal law that dictates what credit repair companies are and are not allowed to do. Many of these companies say they offer legal credit repair, but this is just an advertising tactic to convince desperate consumers to pay money for services that may not help their credit rating at all.

Legitimate credit repair companies operate within the bounds of the CROA. They do not charge you for services they have not completed. They will let you know about your rights to obtain a credit report and dispute inaccurate information on your own. They will send you a contract to review before you agree to the terms and services they may offer. In some cases, you are allowed to cancel your contract within three days of signing it if you change your mind.

Legal credit repair companies don't do anything prohibited by the CROA. This includes lying about the legal credit repair services they provide, asking you to create a new identity, or asking you to waive your rights. Any company like that is certainly not providing legal credit repair. You can report a credit repair company that has broken this law. The Federal Trade Commission is the agency that governs credit repair companies. They have a history of going after credit repair companies that practices any illegal activities.

Your Credit Rights

The Credit Repair Organization Act (CROA) makes it illegal for any credit repair company to lie about what they can actually do for you or charge you before they have performed any services. This law is enforced by the Federal Trade Commission, and it requires credit repair companies to explain your legal rights in a written contract with complete details of the services they will perform. They also need to tell you about your right to cancel within three days without incurring any charges. They should also tell you about the total cost you will pay, and their duty to inform you that how long it will take to get results.

You have a few options if you come across such companies. You can sue them in federal court for your losses (what you paid the company). You can also seek punitive damages, which is the money they have to pay you as a punishment for violating the law. You can join with other consumers who the company also made false promises to and file a class action lawsuit. If you win such a lawsuit the company also has to pay all of your attorney's fees.

DEBT MANAGEMENT

PRACTICAL TIPS IN PERSONAL DEBT MANAGEMENT

If there is one thing that you should learn on your journey to achieve financial freedom, it's debt management. This is not a simple concept that can be mastered overnight. It is something that is learned over time. The outcome will be that you will have more money to save (and spend) and less to be paid towards bad debt.

One of the first things that you should learn is to prioritize your expenses. You should know exactly how much you earn, and from that figure, determine how much will be saved, how much will be spent, and how much will be used to pay for your current bills.

Effective debt management requires the ability to set aside a specific amount of money each billing cycle to pay towards ongoing debts without making unnecessary purchases. While the latest gadgets will make you look cool, managing your debts mean that you will not buy it if you still have obligations if you and you will not buy it if you have to borrow money from someone else to get it.

Debt negotiation is also something you should learn when it comes to debt management. This is not easy because as the name implies, it will require negotiation skills. Nonetheless, with charm and minimal knowledge, you can proceed. You should call the companies where you have existing debts - especially in the case of credit card companies - and ask them if lower interest rates can be offered.

This will be easy if you had been a prompt bill payer and if you never had any problem in the past. Otherwise, it will require a little more push. At the end of the day, debt management is simply all about discipline.

Debt Disciplines:

- Your expenses should be limited to only what you are earn.
- Avoid making unnecessary loans, especially when the sole purpose is luxury.
- Make sure to settle your existing debts first.
- Know where to spend your money and how to spend it wisely.
- Think before buying anything, especially when swiping your credit card.

Keep in mind that debt management will only be successful with a daily dose of discipline.

A GUIDE FOR PERSONAL DEBT MANAGEMENT

If you are carrying a heavy financial burden that you are finding too hard to bear, it would be good to have a personal debt management plan. Through careful management of your financial resources, you can begin to make purchases based only on what you have, not on what you can charge. This will guarantee that you will be able to pay off whatever amount is owed.

Debt Management Habits

Cut down on spending: This is probably the best thing you can do when it comes to debt management. You already have monthly financial obligations to various parties, so there is no need to create more debt before you settle your present obligations. If you cannot have them settled right away, you may end up going into collection, or even legal battles, which can prove to be costly on your part. Make sure that you prioritize your spending. If you have a family, save up for the essentials. Always put your needs above your wants.

Seek help from a lawyer: Managing your personal debt does not mean that you must always take care of everything on your own. There may be situations that prove to be too much for you to handle. In that case, the best thing that you can do is to look for a lawyer to help you with debt settlement. Their legal expertise can be used to help you accomplish your goal of managing your personal debt. Do not attempt to find a resolution for your predicament on your own, especially if you know that you lack the knowledge that you need.

Evaluate your choices carefully: When you are overwhelmed with debt, it might be tempting to take out a loan from a financial institution, an online payday loan company, or borrow money from a friend.

The drawback, however, is that you will have created new debt (with new interest rates) to add to your current debt. Before borrowing money, first think carefully about whether or not it is the best idea. Make sure that all resources are exhausted before you resort to taking out a loan.

It will also be a lot easier if you have the discipline to carefully watch where and how far your money goes. Remember, this is hard-earned money, and you surely don't want it to go waste. The key to financial freedom is managing your finances in the best way possible, which includes living within your means.

In the end, personal debt management can be pretty easy and straightforward if you follow the things that have been previously mentioned.

3 STEPS TO IMPROVE YOUR DEBT MANAGEMENT SKILLS

Improving your skills in debt management is a simple and very rewarding way to pay back loans quicker while paying less interest on money you owe.

Debt is a fundamental part of life and managing it needs to be taken seriously to help avoid problems down the line, including the possibility of having to declare bankruptcy.

All of that can be avoided thereby saving you time, money, and the headache that comes with the stress of outstanding debt.

The easiest way to improve your debt management skills is to follow three simple steps that millions of people do without even thinking about it. Implementing these habits will help you become more disciplined and effective in managing your debt.

1. Never work "debt for debt"

What this means is, don't pay off one debt with another debt source. Some of the most common "debt for debt" payments come in the form of cash advances on credit cards or making payments on a mortgage with a credit card.

Also, never use money set aside for rent or utility bills to pay your creditors. All that is happening is a quick fix that will stretch your debt over years rather than months. So remember, bills first, creditors second.

2. Be realistic about your ability to pay your debts

When the economy and your wallet are in good shape, it's easy to relax your debt disciplines and spend more money. But no matter the circumstances, always have emergency cash on hand and always stick to your goals. Things can go from good to bad in a matter of moments and if you've been buying everything on credit, you could be staring financial ruin right in the face.

When things are going good financially, don't splurge and buy something unnecessary unless you can afford to pay for it in full in cash. Following this rule will prevent you from increasing your debt.

3. Pay high interest-bearing debts first

While it might be tempting to pay off the smallest debt first, the most effective debt management strategy is to go after your highest interest-bearing accounts first. While it might be tempting and seem like a good idea to get rid of the smaller bills first, there are two problems associated with this method.

- Larger debts grow faster than smaller ones, so it makes sense to chip away at the big debts to reduce interest.
- Once you pay off your small debts and get that feeling of accomplishment, you're more likely to take a step backwards to old habits and forget about your debt discipline. Meanwhile those larger debts are still growing.

It might not seem like a big deal but putting off the larger debt to pay later will only cause it to pile up, making it that much harder to pay it off in the end. Improving your debt management skills is an important part of saving you from problems in the future, like bankruptcy and collection creditors.

DEBT MANAGEMENT WITH DEFAULT RISKS

Debt management is difficult to handle because talking about money is always a sensitive issue, especially for those who are in debt. Poverty is neither a crime nor a sin, but many feel ashamed that they are in debt.

If you know someone whose credit suffered because of loan, sticking to simple rules can really help alleviate the pains of bad debt and help them establish good credit. The golden rule is: "Don't ignore your payments. Repay them as soon as possible."

But what happens if you ignore your bills? It seems so harmless at first, to miss a payment or two. You'll just pay it all in one lump sum later, right? This is not a good habit to pick up. It's actually a lot harder than it seems. What happens next is unfortunate and unavoidable.

You see, until you bring the account current – pay all outstanding bills and late fees – the loan continues to become delinquent. If it stays delinquent for 90 days, you will be in default, and the lender will be required to report your delinquency to the three major credit bureaus. That negative credit rating will make it much more difficult for you to borrow money in the future.

I bet you're thinking, "But why are the interest rates so high? I could afford to pay off this loan if I only had to pay back what I borrowed!" In a perfect world, with a perfect use of debt management, this would absolutely be the case. But the truth is, borrowing and lending money is a big business. There's the potential for someone to borrow money, achieve their goal, and quickly pay it off. But more often than not, the person borrowing money takes a lot of time to pay it back, and the loan goes into default.

The thing is, when a borrower defaults, it actually hurts the lender too. A default risk, sometimes referred to as credit risk, can happen on a small or a large scale. Lenders are exposed to these risks because they lent funds with no sign of a return. That's why with each payment, there is a fee (interest).

Generally, there are a lot of ways to manage how much money you've borrowed. The second rule of thumb after the golden rule (pay back your debt as soon as possible) would be to only borrow what you need. Ultimately, the key to successful debt management is to make sure you and your family's needs are met and maintain a good balance between saving, paying current bills, and chipping away at old debt.

CREDIT COUNSELING AGENCIES vs DEBT MANAGEMENT COMPANIES

When your daily mail includes bills marked "Urgent" or "Payment Overdue," and your voicemail box is full of messages from collection agencies, it is probably time for you to seek help.

For many people, this is a difficult step. No one wants to admit that they can't handle their money properly, whether it's to themselves or someone else, especially a stranger.

Credit Counseling Agencies and Debt Management Companies have both worked with hundreds of people who have or have had money problems. They are not going to judge you.

A bit of research can help you decide which one better suit your needs, but basically, the difference between the two is that Credit Counseling Agencies are usually non-profit organizations that advise you on managing your money and debt. Sometimes they offer free credit education workshops.

Debt Management Organizations exist to help you settle your debts with creditors and collectors for a fee. Yes, more often than not, you will have to pay for these services, but if you think about it, you'll agree that the costs are more than worth the peace of mind you will have once you are debt free.

Sample of a Straightforward Pricing Plan:

- *Account set-up fee - Free*
- *Counseling sessions – Free*
- *Monthly service fee - Varies*

Free Educational Materials

Credit Counselors and Debt Managers both want you to learn about money. Any reputable organization will give you free pamphlets and other materials so that you can learn the important aspects of financial planning.

Relationships

Some organizations do not always work well with certain creditors, depending on their history, their clients, and possible conflicts of interest. Make sure any agency or organization that you decide to work with has a reputation of working well with creditors. This will make it easy for you to reach your ultimate goal of becoming debt free with as little drama as possible.

Conclusion

Debt can be a hard thing to get out of and an even harder thing to talk about with someone. The best way to learn is to find the best credit counselor/debt manager for your situation. Doing this is a worthwhile and important first step in dealing with any past creditors and collectors.

Lastly, never be afraid or embarrassed about asking questions. Before jumping in, always make sure you are aware of all their services – which ones are free, and which ones come with a fee. Also, which fees are a one-time charge, and which fees are recurring.

OVERCOME CREDIT DEBT

If you are looking for help with debt, you are not alone. There are many trustworthy credit counseling agencies available. Below are some suggestions:

- The National Foundation for Credit Counseling is a network of local, regional, and national organizations which provide credit, budget, and debt counseling in person, by phone, or online.
- The Association of Independent Consumer Credit Counseling Agencies is a group of independent non-profit agencies that provide credit repair counseling and debt help. These agencies are accredited by the Council on Accreditation.
- Some other sources of help can come from universities, credit unions, housing authorities, and/or military bases. There are branches of the U.S. Cooperative Extension Service which also operate non-profit credit counseling programs.

Any trustworthy credit counseling agency will help you establish and maintain good credit as well as reduce your debt. With a recommended debt management plan and a proper budget, you may be able to reduce interest rates and monthly payments. When you sign up for a debt management plan, make sure it includes your total debt. When you are looking for help to manage your debts, here's what to look for:

- ***Free or low-cost counseling***. There are non-profit credit counseling services which provide free advice about debt, budgeting and credit repair. There is no reason for any agency to charge high fees.

- *A clear understanding of fees.* Do not trust a company that gives you the run-around whenever you inquire about the cost of their services. You should be aware of all the details about an agency and its credit repair plans. Do not surrender your personal details before you know exactly what services they offer, all fees involved, and what is required of you to begin.
- Stay away from business that only offer debt reduction plans. Trustworthy and good agencies offer a variety of services, which include credit repair as well as budget and debt counseling. There are debt management plans in which you make a single payment to the agency which is disbursed to all of your creditors. This will help you get your debts under control and eventually paid off.
- Every agency should take at least an hour to get the details of your financial portfolio. Be ready to bring copies of bills, bank statements and credit reports. Some clients bring bags of statements and bills they have been afraid to open.
- You should be able to get help whether your debts are small or large. Any company requiring a minimum amount of debt to help you, may not be such a good company. Also make sure you check out the agencies you are considering, to see if there have been any complaints about their practices.

FINANCIAL LITERACY

FINANCIAL LITERACY – WHAT IS IT?

Financial literacy is the study of how to make money, how to manage money, how to invest money, and how to donate money to help others. Every adult should learn the secrets behind investing and multiplying their money, and every parent should teach their children how to do the same.

Recent years have seen a growing awareness in financial education as the gateway to improved savings and increased economic security. Efforts to improve financial literacy are now supported by a wide array of organizations, including private employers; state, federal and local government agencies; and consumer groups, community service organizations, commercial banks, and religious organizations.

Financial literacy methods have been implemented across several mediums and have been very effective. Many employers provide financial education, often targeted towards a retirement saving program explained via company seminars, conferences, and the distribution of written information. Secondly, some high schools have implemented mandatory financial, consumer, and/or economics classes that are focused on financial responsibility and record-keeping. Not to mention credit and mortgage counseling agencies that specialize in a one-on-one format that focuses on helping home and business owners manage their debt.

There are also many community-based programs that focus on financial literacy, debt management, budgeting and savings. Often these programs are sponsored through local banks, churches and non-profit organizations.

It is well known that the leading cause of bankruptcy is not always about overspending, or a lack of adequate financial planning. In many cases, the financial free fall is actually the result of a health crisis. In a perfect world, everyone would be fully insured, and insurance would cover everything. But when it doesn't, these issues can also be handled by practicing good financial habits.

That last word there, "habit" is an important word, because one major reason why some people are so bad with money is not because they are financially illiterate, but because of their financial habits. A large part of financial literacy is about getting a better understanding of money and changing your behavior with money. Part of the problem with money is the way it's handled. It's not so much that people are not earning enough money, it's that people have not mastered good financial habits.

FINANCIAL LITERACY: BEING PREPARED FOR THE FUTURE

Part of being prepared to confront the uncertainty of the future is financial education. This kind of education does not require that you go to a university and enroll in formal education - although there are many finance courses that are available. Simply put, financial literacy means that you have an enhanced financial awareness and discipline, which can lead to financial freedom. There are many benefits that can be reaped from financial education, although most of them will not be felt immediately.

With financial education, you will learn how to save. Secondly you will learn how to determine how much you should spend out of what you earn. A good habit to start is to set aside your savings first and use whatever remains for your expenses.

Additionally, part of your savings should include investing. Some people are content with putting their money in a savings account at their bank. However, you may run the risk of depreciation in the value of currency and minimal interest rates.

Therefore, a better alternative would be to put some funds in diversified stock investments. One of the principles of finance states that the return will be higher if there are more risks involved. Therefore, if the investment is risky, your money may grow in significant ways.

Being educated financially also means that you will know which items deserve your money and which ones do not. You will know if it is worth it to splurge on a vacation, a new car, or a new house. Or not.

There are federal and state laws that govern education at every level, beginning with teaching people how to read, how to write, and how to count. It is unfortunate that financial education is not part of mandatory curriculum. If it were, people would learn how to manage their personal finances early on, which would equip them with tools to prevent them from being broke in the future. They would be ready to face any financial turbulence in the global economy.

In conclusion, it pays to have financial literacy. You will reap long-term benefits and create a positive impact in your life. Truly, financial education is one of the key ingredients to a better and happier future, where financial freedom can be enjoyed.

THE SIGNIFICANCE OF FINANCIAL EDUCATION

In the absence of sound financial planning, big problems can arise, especially the inability to sustain one's daily needs. There is no doubt that financial education is necessary, especially for the younger generation who is still learning about responsibility when it comes to money. If you are financially literate, you will find it easier to weigh the pros and cons of investment opportunities. You will also find it easier to comprehend any possible investment risks.

Here are some ways financial literacy can improve your life:

Budgeting: Financial literacy is a big help when it comes to being able to create a budget and stick to it. This is especially true if you are the kind of person with a limited amount of money who has a lot of expenses, such as mortgage, transportation, children, and other daily essentials. If you are financially literate, you will find it easy to manage your cash flow and live within your means.

Financial Security: No one knows what the future holds. Today you could have thousands of dollars in your savings account and six months from now, not know where your next paycheck is coming from. Financial education will help you prepare for the worst by setting up an emergency fund. This will guard you against unforeseen expenses in the future regarding your household, vehicles, and health. In addition to an account for emergency funds, you can also set up other funds for education, vacation, and holiday expenses.

With the economic turbulence being experienced by so many in this country, it is prudent to consider improving your financial literacy. It may be harder to live within you means, especially with the cost of living increasing and unemployment on the rise, but it can be done. With financial literacy, it is possible for you to manage whatever uncertainty the future may hold.

LAND BANKING

LAND BANKING: A TRADITIONAL WAY OF INVESTING

If you have not heard about land banking in the past, consider yourself lucky as this section will provide you with new insights that can prove to be very helpful in enhancing your knowledge. With land banking, you simply invest your money in a piece of land, hoping that the investment will yield favorable returns. Given the current economic situation and the problems within the real estate industry, there are many who have doubts if land banking is still a relevant option. However, being an expert in the field of real estate, trust me, it still proves to be one of the most favorable forms of investing in the market.

When it comes to land banking, there are certain factors to keep in mind about how to locate a piece of land that will be profitable.

The following are three factors that you should consider:

Population Growth: Whether the economy is in a recession or progression, you can expect that people will still be looking for new homes. A good land banking strategy would be to buy land in an area where there is considerable population growth, which means there will be a high demand for land. Make sure to forecast the trends and buy while the prices are still low.

Unemployment Rate: When the unemployment rate is high, that means that there will be fewer people that can afford to spend money on a new home. Therefore, another good land banking strategy is to buy land in locations where the unemployment rate is low.

Taxes: There are serious challenges in this area. Tax delinquent properties pose problems which may not be publicly known. A growing number of empty properties can lead to a decline, not only in government revenues (taxes), but also in communities. It is also important to find the correct owners of abandoned properties because land without a title can be very troublesome for a perspective buyer.

Neglect: Other issues faced by property developers include owners who neglect their property, which causes it to deteriorate and decline in value. Not maintaining property you own is against law.

Foreclosures: In some land property foreclosures, the rightful owners are not even known. This can cause problems like the time and cost of recovery, and other practical problems like criminals using empty plots and abandoned homes. There are some solutions to put the unused properties to potentially good use.

It is good if you understand and evaluate all possible barriers before investing in any property. Evaluate all inventory and make sure that you are aware of all tax foreclosure statutes. Foreclosure is basically all the legal proceedings initiated by a bank or creditor to claim the loan for which no return or premium was paid. There is usually a short time period between delinquency and foreclosure.

Community: Lastly you should also consider the condition of the community to make sure that there is room for progress in the future.

There is no doubt that investing your money in a piece of land can prove to be favorable in the end. However, this will only be the case when you choose the land wisely. When things are done cautiously and risks are properly calculated, you can be confident that land banking will work at your advantage.

SAVING TOOLS

Many people see saving as a tedious chore. It's hard to save when you spend more than you make. Now this view is from the standpoint of someone who has kept their Nine to Five job. I've been employed with a local bus company for over twenty years.

When I first started, I was looking for easy wins. I wanted my business to pay my cell phone bill each month. Then it was my cell phone bill and my cable bill. Eventually my business grew a life of its own. I also gauged my success by seeing how much money I could save from my regular paycheck.

Now I enjoy arching my money – studying ways to put my money to work and watching it grown. You can't take advantage of an opportunity if you have no capital to use.

Employer Savings Plans

When I began my business, I was able to utilize tools I already had in place. I used the advisory tools that my company provided. Many companies have savings plans. My favorite program allows for long term growth with the ability to liquidate your assets if needed. There are also short-term tools that you can access right through your home computer.

DIY vs Professionals

I am not a fan of DIY when it comes to money. People who have cash pay people to give them sound advice. I beg of you to do the same. Hiring someone can help take the decision-making power out of your hands which will avoid unneeded stress. Forget your educational level or degree unless it's in personal finances.

Savings Accounts

When it comes to savings accounts, your local bank can help with that. You may be able to find an online bank that will offer specials to open a savings account. Begin by saving small amounts of your paycheck until your business generate real income.

What is business income?

Many people think that if they sell a product and make $100.00, that's their profit or revenue. The question is, what and how much did it take for you to make that $100.00? What were the ingredients to formulate that money?

What is your time worth? Understanding your time is the most important tool you can have. My rate runs between $85.00 to $100.00 per hour, depending on the task. I also have clients who pay me thousands per month to be able to speak with me. In the beginning, making money is hard. Finding that sweet spot for your services is challenging. Are you pricing yourself too low or too high? These are the reasons why knowing your worth is essential.

Certificates of Deposit

The next savings tool I would like to mention is CDs. CD's work great whether you're saving for the short-term or the long-term . If you have capital that you won't be using for at least six months, consider a CD. While the interest may be nothing compared to your deposits, you can still make money.

Taxes

Many Americans have some form of income to report annually on their tax return. Tax season is the best time of year to start your business, as you have funds readily available. You can use your tax refund to purchase a new computer or pay a year's worth of business expenses in advance. Doing this frees up future capital for you to use to expand at a later date. You can also use your refund to make an annual payment on one or more of your bills. Like your car insurance for example. Doing this may generate a discount on your policy. So, while it may feel hurtful to pay a huge chunk of money upfront, the long-term effects can bring additional cash into your business.

Credit Cards

I wouldn't tell anyone to grow their business on credit cards. You may use credit cards for large one-time purchases so that you can avoid paying for them over time and being charged interest. Please be careful of interest rates and other rate increases by the credit card corporations. Use your cards sparingly and have a plan in place to pay them off in full once the bill arrives.

In Conclusion:

What are you planning to give up in order to go up? What are you willing to sacrifice for your dreams? For me it was sleep. It was leisure time. It was understanding that everything I do has a purpose. Getting up in the morning, putting on that uniform, driving that bus in the cold, all of that was well worth the gains I received. Often I spend time away from friends and family and many times I cut down on entertainment to complete a task. I even worked through my breaks to write this book. I gave it all up.

What are you willing to give up in order to go up?

LEAVING YOUR NINE-TO-FIVE

TO LEAVE OR NOT TO LEAVE? THAT IS THE QUESTION

When to leave your "Nine to Five" is a question every entrepreneur and new business owner asks themselves at one time or another.

Projected income versus reality income will definitely come into play if you are starting a business. While this looks true on the surface, it isn't. Instead of working for someone else, you will be working for yourself. If you have a family business, you may be working for them.

Building your business can be a daunting feat. A family buy-in is a unique way to begin. Family buy-ins come in many different forms. A family must stay connected throughout this venture. Your partner or spouse may be helping with the kids, and the kids may be helping both of you with small business tasks. In many cases, the good adventures of a family business will out weight the bad. Most families seek assurances that their lifestyles won't change. Owning a business and living in poverty is not what most have in mind. If there are two incomes, maybe allowing one partner to continue working isn't such a bad idea, but you don't want one person to feel that they're responsible for the whole shebang. It's essential to review your financial goals through the transition from traditional employment to business ownership.

Successful implementation of "Assurance Business Practices" can reduce the stress on family members not involved in the business. Accountability is of the utmost importance. How can you make your family feel secure while this transition is happening? Including your family in business decisions that directly affect them is one way.

Family members want assurances the bills will be paid. They want to make sure healthcare remains the same. Living under the pressure of late mortgage payments and the stress that can bring is not a healthy environment, especially in a marriage. Most professional partners desire a home environment where they can thrive.

As your business grows, making sure your bills are paid on time is important. If you cannot "pay life" on time, what do you expect your payroll to look like? Understanding a budget isn't just filling in a spreadsheet but having a full working knowledge of the timeline of your bills.

Having an open line of communication with your family – whether it's your children or your spouse – is also important because everyone must buy into the idea of supporting the family business. There will be lean times when everyone has to pitch in and save money. Talking about this in advance and being aware of the goals that need to be met will lessen the stress when those lean times come. As with any relationship, communication is key.

You may ask, will I have time for fun? Scheduling fun time will allow you to recharge. I schedule a vacation every six weeks and go somewhere different to recharge and reflect. I'm not saying drop everything and run (remember you are the boss), just try to allow for a healthy amount of time to rest your body and your mind.

You can attend meetings from the shore for a few minutes, and then enjoy the rest of the day at the beach. There's nothing wrong with answering emails at the coffee shop, just remember not to be reclusive with your family while you're away. It's important to spend time enjoying the fruits of your labor. I'm a spendthrift at heart. For example, I'll schedule a business meeting while in Florida. This allows me to write off the trip. (You may need to consult a tax attorney for the correct wording for these types of business practices.)

What freedoms come from owning your business? For many, escaping from underneath the traditional "Nine to Five" job is number one. Using your body as a tool when growing your business should not be overlooked. As a business owner, you set your schedule for the times that make you feel most comfortable. While many choose to sleep whenever they want, real entrepreneurs schedule their rest. My schedule is not typical or traditional, and that's okay. I find that working in the middle of the night is my most productive period. My best advice: make sure you create a schedule that works for you and don't forget to schedule in time to sleep.

While it takes courage to own your own business, many people only see the freedom it can bring. Courage comes in all forms. The ability to persuade family and friends that your idea is worthwhile is courageous. Telling your family you're leaving your traditional job definitely takes courage.

Many family members have ideas of where and what you are supposed to be in life. Parents tend to impose their dreams on their children. Being able to tell your parents that you want to follow your own dream takes more courage than you think. While all of our parents want us to be successful, success means something different to everyone.

Protecting Your Business

INTRODUCTION

Many people turn their business ideas into jobs. Businesses are the creativity of great thinkers. Using your skills to put together a plan for success is where the rubber meets the road. Most people want to protect their business at any cost. They say, "My business is my baby." Babies grow up, become kids, then adults. Are you treating your business like an infant and keeping it in that stage? If there is no growth in your business, why are you still operating?

There are many reasons a business does not grow. One of the main reasons is poor business management. This is why protecting your business is so important. You don't want to leave your business open to attacks.

Types of Attacks on Your Business

Self-sabotage will tear your business apart. Not being focused and not keeping your guard up are two ways your business can be ruined. Knowing the ins and outs of your industry is paramount to the success and protection of your business. Many people enter a field and never bother to learn (much less keep up with) new techniques, technologies, and tricks of the trade. The industry that I've built my businesses on require continual educational sacrifices.

Daily Business Rituals

My daily business rituals are as follows: I'm up by 8:00 am. While I'm getting ready, I usually listen to motivational lectures on YouTube. After showering, I listen to 15 minutes of World News. In my business, news is important. Many people say they don't like the news, but how else will you learn about worldwide business trends? Learning to appreciate information is critical to protecting your business.

TYPES OF INSURANCE

People have long since desired to care for themselves, their family, their possessions, and their businesses and they found a pretty simple option to life's unpredictable situations and problems: insurance. The oldest and most popular companies are Aetna Inc., State Farm Group, and American Insurance Group.

The insurance market consists of the following subcategories: Life Insurance, Medical Insurance, Pension Insurance, Savings Insurance, Commercial Insurance, and the most popular type, **Personal Insurance**.

Liability or Casualty Insurance is coverage when a person or object of value is reimbursed due to damages.

Vehicle Insurance is presupposed by the law regardless of the state you live in. It is senseless to think that when getting into a car accident, an insurance company of another person will cover your damages. Every state has its own rules and laws. Your policy with the auto insurance company will secure you against various types of accidents. If you drive with no insurance, it is against the law and you will be heavily charged.

Health Insurance ranks second among types of insurance and can be considered one of the most important since it enhances our lives by health prevention and intervention. Whenever you wish to visit a doctor, your health insurance is your first line of defense.

Life Insurance is viewed by some as the inheritance you leave for the ones you left behind after you die. This type of insurance is extremely important if you are the only provider in the family and your family will have no livelihood if something happens to you. These policies provide support for your family from being able to cover funeral expenses to giving them the financial support they need after your death.

SMALL BUSINESS INSURANCE ISSUES

Business insurance protects the business owner, the business, and in certain cases the employees. This protection could be used as supplemental income during a period of restoration or as financial aid to repair a business after a disaster. Insurances like Workers' Compensation can protect your company from lawsuits and provide financial compensation to any employee injured on the job.

Expenses Involved

If a small business has employees, then by law the employer must purchase certain types of insurance, such as Workers' Compensation. Starting and running any business can be an expensive venture, and purchasing insurance adds more to the list. Every business owner should take some steps to ensure that they get the most for their money and also save some wherever possible.

Insurance brokers aid shop around for the best rates and help you select the best coverage. Before you work with a broker, it is recommended that you do your own shopping; it will be beneficial for you if you find the names of brokers or companies which specialize in your type of business beforehand. You can also save money on your policy if you elect to pay a higher deductible when you file a claim, which will definitely lower what you have to pay in premiums.

Insufficient Coverage

Most standard policies adequately cover small businesses, but certain industries benefit from specialty or additional business insurance coverage. All business owners are recommended to consult with an insurance broker in advance to ensure that they have sufficient coverage in their insurance policies.

The Insurance Information Institute cites a case in which a dry cleaner did not have enough coverage in his standard business owner's policy to handle a $54 million lawsuit. If the dry cleaner lost the lawsuit, it would quickly bankrupt his business. I stand behind the sentiment that "No business can ever afford to be unprepared for a lawsuit."

To prevent any such scenario you may want to add features to your current policy or purchase additional policies.

Claims

Filing a claim is sometimes necessary for a company to recoup after a loss and/or protect your remaining assets. However, claims can also be disputed. For example, your claim might be denied, or you may feel as though the compensation you received is not enough to cover your loss. But remember, the insurance company compensates you according to your policy, not your need. To minimize disagreements over a claim, you should always be prepared with your own records and research. It is suggested that all business owners should record their business activity and the expenses it takes to keep their business operating in a temporary location during the period of disruption.

If you are not able to resolve your issue with the adjuster, you can speak with the manager of customer service for the insurance company. If all these measures fail, you can talk to your state's banking and insurance department or as a last option to an attorney. Remember if your claim was denied that does not always mean that the insurance company is wrong, there might be other issues.

BUSINESS INSURANCE

THE NEED FOR BUSINESS INSURANCE

Having business insurance is a must, but there are many people who are skeptical about getting coverage. Running a business is not a piece of cake. More often than not, you need to exert extra effort if you want to craft a success story for your endeavors. There are many things that should be given attention. For instance, you need to think about your marketing strategies and future developments that will offer your clientele something new. And of course, you need to have insurance for whatever business it is that you operate.

Some people might think that business insurance is an unnecessary expense. While it is true that it is an expense for your business, it is a necessary one because of the many benefits that it provides. Once you start your business, you should keep in mind that there will be a need for certain expenditures, and business insurance should be included.

One of the most important reasons for getting business insurance is that it is a legal requirement. Many states require businesses to have insurance, which will provide them with the ability to cover whatever problems arise in their company. If a business fails get coverage, it could lead to the forfeiture of their license to operate and other legal consequences.

If you use vehicles for your business, it is also important that they are insured. This will spare you from financial responsibility when accidents happen, especially accidents that involve other parties.

In the event that your company is sued, business insurance can help you settle the demands of various claims, such as "failure to act in accordance with a signed contract between two parties."

If your business is a brick-and-mortar one, business insurance will also prove to be helpful if there is a fire on the premises. If you have coverage, the insurer will provide you with financial assistance to the extent that it is covered by the premium being paid. This is also true in cases of theft, and other situations.

At the end of the day, while it is indeed true that having insurance means spending more, it is still necessary for business protection and security, especially given the fact that the future is very uncertain. Make sure to be as discerning as possible in choosing a company where you will get the best coverage at a rate that works best for you.

BUSINESS OWNER INSURANCE PACKAGES

Throwing off the shackles of employee life and embracing the DIY of running a small home business can be an amazing thing. You get to set your own hours, you're free to leave the workplace (home) whenever you please, and you can (hopefully) make a lot more money.

But as they say, with great power, comes great responsibility (or, in this case, with a home business, comes possible financial disaster).

Insurance is one of the most important things to have with any small business, home-based or otherwise, in case of problems or accidents, including:

- Personal injury, stopping you from running your business
- Theft or damage of equipment or property required to run your business
- Damage to other people or property due to your service or products
- Injury to your employees (if applicable)
- Other potential business-related problems that can occur

Once you start looking at having multiple insurance policies, they can add up to quite a bit; even if you shop around for the cheapest rates for different coverage, you will end up having to juggle tons of bills, account managers and institutions, making your work harder than it needs to be.

So how do you get around these problems?

Introducing the BOP

A BOP, or Business Owners Package, is the solution!

It is more or less an insurance "package" that caters to SBO's (small business owners), and includes all of the essential policies every SBE (small business enterprise) should have:

- Property and Equipment Insurance
- Business and Personal Insurance
- Advertising Coverage (copyright infringement and slander)

Not only does this help roll all your policies into a single package, but the institution that provides the coverage will usually provide you with a premium rate.

The basics of these packages are outstanding. They provide flexibility and cost effectiveness in a single package that is simple to understand and manage.

But what if "the basics" aren't enough for your situation?

Bring on the Add-ons

Most institutions will allow you to customize your policies by adding extra coverage on top of the existing policy, helping to keep everything below cost and easily manageable.

Depending on your specific needs and industry, you may need to include certain policies, such as:

- Errors & Omission Insurance helps protect you from lawsuits claiming you made a mistake in your professional services.
- Workers' Compensation covers death, injury, or accidents suffered by workers in the course of their employment and paid to them or their dependents.

- Health and disability insurance is intended to replace some of a working person's income when a disability prevents them from working. It does not cover medical care or long-term care services.
- Business auto insurance provides coverage for a company's use of cars, trucks, vans, and other vehicles in the course of carrying out its business.

While health and disability only cover you, by rolling them in with your existing BOP, you receive greater benefits that cover you, your business, and your employees.

Final Thoughts

The easiest and cheapest way to protect your business is to find an institution that can offer you a BOP.

A package can turn out to be much cheaper than buying separate policies, and easier to update and track your coverage. You can bundle other policies into your BOP as needed and all for a discounted price!

Look for an institution that gives you this option and there will never be any insurance issues that you cannot face for your business.

INVEST A LITTLE MORE IN YOUR INVESTMENT

When you have already invested everything you have in your business, where do you go when you need more financial help in a disaster? And remember crisis can strike anytime, anywhere and in any form. It does not matter if you own a small business or a big company, insurance will keep your business safe.

Some people prefer health or property insurances over business insurance. There are many small businesses that are still uninsured. Business insurance provides coverage from any loss in business during its normal course. The type of business insurance you need depends on employees, financial risks, property value, extent of damage or loss. A good insurance company and broker can advise you about the category of insurance you should select.

Types of Business Insurance:

- General Liability Insurance covers legal costs in case of body injury, property damage, medical expenses and all other judicial procedures.
- Product Liability Insurance is for manufacturing companies and their stake in the product. In the manufacturing line any defected product is a liability.
- Professional Liability Insurance is for service providers, like doctors who need malpractice insurance. This is sometimes called Omission & Error Insurance.
- Commercial Property Insurance can protect your business in instances of fire, flood, or crime.
- Home-Based Business Insurance provides general and business liability coverage for your home-based business that your homeowner insurance does not cover.

- Flood Insurance covers your property when a flood has caused damage to your business. Unfortunately, property and casualty insurance does not cover natural disasters like floods.
- Windstorm Insurance protects your home and business against wind. Wind damage can be caused by items being blown and destroying your property as a result. However, this type of coverage is limited to states where hurricanes and tornadoes are common.

Every insurance company has different risk assessment techniques. They consider your application and decide whether they will provide all of the requested cover or a part of it. Decide on the amount of premiums, deductible and claims beforehand. When you make a claim there is a certain amount of money you need to pay, this is called the deductible. So, it is crucial that you asses all your risks and look around and inquire into a few companies before settling with one insurer.

Remember your valuable employees and get them insured as well. There is insurance for a valuable person in your organization, called key person or keyman insurance. This employee is responsible for the profit for your company, so, if that employee decides to leave, you will have some financial security for your expected losses as a result of their departure.

Make sure you find a good broker, who is experienced, licensed and has a good reputation. Remember that some rates and policies will depend on the size of your company. It is important that you analyze your insurance policy annually. With time your business may grow along with your assets, so keep your insurance policies in check and in accordance with your business growth.

CASUALTY & PROPERTY INSURANCE

PROPERTY INSURANCE IS A MUST

Not many business owners are aware of the importance of property insurance. Many think it's an expense that won't reap rewards in the future. Contrary to this belief, this kind of insurance is a must.

One of the reasons you should purchase property insurance is that it is required by the lender as part of the mortgage if you have a brick-and-mortar business. It's the same as homeowner's insurance. Regardless of the effort you exert to keep your house safe, the time will come when the inevitable happens. For instance, a natural disaster could destroy your home. If you don't have insurance, it will be very hard for you to handle the reconstruction that will be needed, especially if you are short in terms of financial resources. However, if you have property insurance, you will be covered. The insurer will cover the expenses that are needed.

Legal protection is another benefit that is sometimes included with property insurance. There is liability coverage for homeowner's insurance that will provide you with a legal shield when the unexpected happens.

For instance, if you have a dog as a household pet and it bites your neighbor, you could be sued for negligence. In turn, the insurance can protect you from a legal perspective, including the possibility of paying for the medical expenses of the party that has been injured. In the absence of insurance, you will be solely responsible to settle the medical bills and any other expenses associated with the incident.

At the end of the day, property insurance is definitely relevant, especially in the uncertain times we live in. Make sure you find a reputable insurer, get a policy with sufficient coverage, and a premium that you can afford.

CASUALTY & PROPERTY INSURANCE CONSIDERATIONS

Research: This is one of the most critical factors that will impact your decision when purchasing casualty insurance. It may be a tedious process to go online and browse through reviews that have been shared by other people about a specific insurance company, or to ask people you know personally if they can recommend an insurance company to you. However, doing these things will prove to be worth the time and the effort. Doing this will provide you with the opportunity to weigh the pros and cons about available options various companies have to offer.

Budget: The premium that you pay for casualty insurance will depend on how much you have allotted in your budget for that expense. It will also depend on the frequency of the payments.

To avoid having your insurance be a financial burden, make sure that the premium is something that your budget can handle with ease. After all, you would not want to end up being broke because of insurance.

Management: In every institution, management has played a key role in boosting growth. Likewise, when choosing a property and casualty insurance company, you should consider the stability of its management. Insurance investments survive by investing with borrowed money. Therefore, if the company's management is not reputable, then it's not advisable for you to invest in it.

You should also check on the management's impact on the shareholder's value benefits. Usually, the best companies offer long term remuneration policies that advance shareholders' returns.

Investments

When choosing the right property and casualty insurance company, it is important to review their investment policies. Though some insurers' income profiles are private, that's not the case for all. You should look at areas such as: Credit ratings, periods of fixed income portfolio, and the split between bonds and equity. By checking a company's historical data, you can be fully convinced that the company won't have a history of insufficiency.

A property and casualty insurance company may be a great area for you to invest in. It is more complex compared to other insurance companies. Now you have enough knowledge and confidence to choose the best company for you. Remember, it is important to survey different companies and understand their basics in terms of management, reserves, investments, underwriting and evaluation.

PROPERTY ISSUES

Since the great recession of 2007 housing and property prices in the U.S. have gradually declined, which happened due to decreased demand. In 2012, there were speculations about an impending economic bubble.

Property or real estate bubbles occur every now and then in local and international property markets. An economic bubble is a time period over which there is a rapid rise in the market price of particular property until it reaches a certain level. Then the bubble pops and the price of the property starts declining rapidly.

In spite of all this, if you still buy property then there are additional problems you might face. You won't just require the startup costs but there may be additional remodeling costs after you have closed the deal on your new property. If you are going to own and operate a piece of property for your business, you will need to set aside money for repairs. Many things like plumbing, wiring, paint, flooring will need to be updated at some point and time.

It is important that you maintain your property and keep your property insured. Keeping your property secure is not only legally compulsory but also good for your own safety. Remember to install a good security system and also keep all the codes handy, you might need them in case of emergency. If someone is injured during an incident on your property they may try to sue you, so maintenance is important.

Paying property tax is mandatory. However, buying any additional property is only advisable if you have attained a certain level of financial independence.

THREE WAYS TO LOWER HOMEOWNER'S INSURANCE

Wouldn't you love to be able to lower your homeowner's insurance? While it's certainly a necessary insurance policy to have (most mortgage companies won't give out a mortgage without one) they can be expensive, hitting up to $1000 in low-risk areas and 10 times that in high-risk areas (prone to earthquakes floods, storms, etc.).

Homeowners insurance might be expensive but there are some sure-fire ways to lower your annual premiums and save for that vacation or new dish washer. Take these three ways to lower your homeowner's insurance and you will see a huge difference.

1. Have a working security system and smoke detector

An easy way to lower your homeowner's insurance premium is to install a security system that is either monitored by a security company or linked directly to the police and have smoke alarms and other fire protection within the house.

A sophisticated security system can lower your premiums by up to 15% annually depending on the reputation of the company. Always remember to keep the quote from the installation or grab a recent bill and take it to your insurer as proof to receive the deduction.

A smoke alarm in homes can lower your premium, especially in older homes, by 10% annually. Generally, a photo or quick inspection will help you receive the benefits of having these installed in your home.

Installing things like automatic leak detectors, battery backup systems for sump pumps, and lighting protection systems can all help to chip away at those engorged premiums.

2. Increase your deductible

Another quick and easy way to lower your homeowner's insurance is to increase the deductible on the policy.

The average deductible is in the range of $500 to $1000 (depending on the value of the house) but going for minimum deductibles isn't the smart way to work.

Increase your deductible to the higher end of the spectrum, like $2,500, $5,000 or even $10,000 and you will see a massive drop in your annual premiums.

It might sound scary, but the best way to decide your 'perfect deductible' is to take into account your income, savings and how much you are willing to pay on general repairs. You are better off paying the technician to fix the rotten door or broken window and save hundreds or thousands in annual premiums.

This is one of the easiest ways to lower your *homeowner's insurance* drastically and stay in the good books with your insurer.

3. Look for discounts on multiple policies

Most companies offer discounts if you hold more than one insurance policy under their roof (the discount would apply to BOTH policies).

Talk to your *homeowner's insurance* holder about multiple policy discounts and consider changing your health or auto insurance over to your current insurer. Most companies will offer to lower your *homeowner's insurance* and health or auto by as much as 10% or 15%, saving you a fortune on both premiums.

Conclusion

These 3 steps can benefit you in a big way. By installing protection systems in your home, increasing your deductible and bundling packages together, you can **lower your** *homeowner's insurance* premiums to a very manageable price.

LAND BANKING INSURANCE

Investing in vacant land without liability insurance is a dangerous thing to own! Trespassing or not, you will be liable for every person that enters onto your grounds. You will also be liable for any injuries caused to them, damages caused to someone else's property, and subsequent lawsuits that may follow.

People involved in *land banking* are extremely susceptible to lawsuits like this. Whether you're just starting to build your portfolio, or you are experienced in *land banking*, don't leave yourself open with vacant land without liability insurance; problems could be right around the corner!

What does it cover?

Liability insurance covers you for damages sustained by a person on your property or damage to another person's property because of your own.

Liability insurance on a vacant lot will help to cover all legal costs that are involved in any lawsuits, as well as any reimbursements owed to the plaintiff up to your maximum coverage.

Owning vacant land without liability insurance can become a very costly as you can see by the examples below.

General coverage rates

Most vacant land can be covered for a range of rates, including:

- $100,000 per occurrence, $300,000 aggregate
- $250,000 per occurrence, $500,000 aggregate
- $500,000 per occurrence, $1 million aggregate
- $1 million per occurrence, $2 million aggregate

These are just basic limits that should provide adequate cover for a regular owner, but someone involved in *land banking* might need to look at getting umbrella coverage, which can cover someone for up to $100 million.

When is it essential to invest?

There are quite a few scenarios when liability for vacant land is necessary:

- If you own large plots of land that can be used for hunting or fishing and intend to let people on the land, liability insurance can help cover you in case of any accidents that can occur during regular use.
- ATV users and hikers can also be a big liability. Many things can happen, including damage due to other hikers, faulty structures and plants and animals. Liability insurance should cover most of these. Also check for building coverage on the property.
- Unwarranted foot traffic can be a big problem for vacant land without liability insurance, especially if the land is in the middle of a busy city/suburban area and is a short cut to local areas. People are always going to walk through and if people happen to get injured while walking through, or they throw a lit cigarette that causes a fire that damages other buildings, you will be liable for all the damages.

Conclusion

While vacant land without liability insurance isn't the most important thing to have in the world, if there's a good chance people are likely to use your land for whatever reason, then this insurance is for you.

Land banking will certainly open you up to these problems (owning multiple lots, especially in high-traffic areas, could open you up to potential lawsuits) and having any vacant land without liability insurance is an option not worth taking.

WHEN DISASTER STRIKES

Disasters can cause damage to your property and it takes a significant financial toll on those who experience this. Do not be confused on how to handle claims, what to do before and after a disaster and your insurance coverage information.

When your property is destroyed or damaged, you will have many questions and be faced with various decisions. Disasters are unforeseen and unpredictable.

Most likely you will have concerns about emergency repairs, temporary shelter, and the costs of restoring or rebuilding your property. This can be very overwhelming.

Before Disaster Strikes

It is very crucial to have some type of insurance coverage for your personal belongings and property. If you rent an apartment, your landlord might ensure the building you live in, but the landlord's insurance will not cover your personal belongings.

To make claim handling a little easier, here are some things you can do before any disaster strikes:

- Inventory your personal property. Record the serial and model numbers for items like TVs, DVRs, computers, etc. Retaining the receipts for these items is also helpful.
- Consider taking pictures or make a video recording of the items inside your home. Also keep the Inventory records at a location other than your insured home.
- Making photocopies of your insurance policy and keeping the copies in a secure location away from your residence is also a great idea.
- Keeping electronic copies of important papers and telephone numbers readily available in case of an emergency is important.

- You should be familiar with the coverage of your property's insurance policy. Making sure that you understand the difference between replacement cost coverage for your contents and their actual cash value (ACV) is good for you. ACV can replace contents at cost minus depreciation.
- This way, replacement cost will replace your contents at today's current prices.
- Always remember that any basic homeowners' insurance policy does not cover floods, earthquakes or mine subsidence damages. Coverage for these disasters can be added later to your insurance policy for additional premium. You can contact your insurance producer for further information.

After Disaster Strikes

- After a disaster strikes you should contact your insurance company as soon as possible and provide as many details as you can about the damage to your property.
- Call your insurance company directly and ask for the claims department.
- The company's contact number can be obtained through the Department of Insurance and it is always listed in your policy. Be sure that you provide all your phone numbers where you may be reached, especially when your home is uninhabitable. Your insurance company will definitely need to contact you.
- It is very important that you fully understand your rights and responsibilities, in order to take charge of your situation. If your insurance policy has been destroyed or lost in the disaster or if you are confused about the policy benefits or exclusions, just ask your insurance producer or company exactly what coverage you have paid for. Ask for copy of your policy.

HEALTH INSURANCE

HEALTH INSURANCE PROGRAMS

The most common types of insurance programs are the following:

Policy for Unemployed Individuals

For those people who have recently lost their job, there is a special program called COBRA (The Consolidated Omnibus Budget Reconciliation Act). COBRA offers the same health insurance coverage for these individuals that they had when they were employed. However, the biggest drawback of this policy is that the premiums are paid by the individual instead of the company.

Policy for Self-employed Individuals

Self-employed people must purchase a personal health insurance policy offered by a great number of reputable companies. There is always a choice, which allows any person to select the most appropriate plan according to their budget and preferences.

Medicare

Currently the USA government offers alternative health insurance programs for people who are older than 65 years and invalids of younger ages are able to obtain Medicare if they have been approved for disability benefits from Social Security.

Medicaid

Medicaid is a federal and state program that helps with healthcare costs for some people with limited income and resources. Medicaid also offers benefits not normally covered by Medicare.

TYPES OF HEALTH INSURANCE PLANS

When it comes to shopping for health insurance, you will notice that there are many companies that offer different types of plans. They range from bronze, silver, gold, and platinum. The bronze plan offers the least amount of coverage and the platinum plan offers the most.

Insurance companies such as Cigna, Humana, Kaiser and United may offer one or more of these types of plans. Therefore, when choosing health insurance, it's important to learn about the different brands so you will select the plan that will meet your needs.

Below is a summary of different insurance brands.

Health Maintenance Organizations (HMO)

HMO stands for health maintenance organization. HMOs have their own network of doctors, hospitals and other healthcare providers who have agreed to accept payment at a certain level for any services they provide. This allows the HMO to keep costs in check for its members.

Preferred Provider Organization (PPO)

A PPO health plan contracts with medical providers, such as hospitals and doctors, to create a network of participating providers. You pay less if you use providers that belong to the plan's network.

PPOs generally offer greater flexibility in seeing specialists, have larger networks than HMOs, and offer some out-of-network coverage.

Point of Service Plan (POS)

The Point of Service plan combines features of HMOs and PPOs. With POS, you are given the freedom to choose health insurance providers of their choice. You may also have a primary doctor whom you refer to when using network providers. When using out of network providers, you will be charged more for medical services. In POS plans, the premiums are low since the deductibles are high. Higher deductibles are experienced when one chooses to use out of network providers. When using out of network providers, you have to pay the medical bill up front and then submit a claim to your POS plan provider so that you can be compensated.

Health Savings Account (HSA)

A type of savings account that lets you set aside money on a pre-tax basis to pay for qualified medical expenses. By using untaxed dollars in an HSA to pay for deductibles, copayments, coinsurance, and some other expenses, you may be able to lower your overall health care costs.

High Deductibles Health Plan (HDHP)

A high-deductible health plan is a health insurance plan with lower premiums and higher deductibles than a traditional health plan. It is intended to incentivize consumer-driven healthcare. Being covered by an HDHP is also a requirement for having a health savings account.

For 2019, the IRS defines a high deductible health plan as any plan with a deductible of at least $1,350 for an individual or $2,700 for a family. ... An HDHP's total yearly out-of-pocket expenses (including deductibles, copayments, and coinsurance) can't be more than $6,900 for an individual or $13,800 for a family.

If you're in good health, rarely need prescription drugs, and don't expect to incur significant medical expenses in the coming year, you might consider an HDHP. In trade for lower premiums, HDHPs require you meet your deductible before you get any coverage for treatment other than preventive care.

HOW TO SAVE MONEY WITH HEALTH INSURANCE

With the high rise of economy in the US, citizens have found it hard to pay for health insurance since the premiums and co-pays tend to be too high while the wages have remained stagnant. Nonetheless, high costs should not be an excuse for not having health insurance. Whether you are single or have a family, medical coverage should be your first priority. As a result, there are a couple of things to consider when it comes to health insurance that may save you a few dollars in the long run.

Choose a plan that best suits you. Usually when choosing a plan with lower premiums, the co-pays are higher than plans with more expensive premiums. By choosing a cheaper plan, you can calculate the annual costs of your co-pays, premiums and other out-of-the-bracket costs you might use during the plan year. However, you may find yourself saving more money in the long run.

Take part in your employer's health insurance plan. Usually employers are able to receive more favorable rates from insurance companies since they deal with large volumes of people seeking insurance coverage. By doing this, they get a discount which their employees can take advantage when the Annual Open Enrollment season begins.

Avoid the emergency room. Usually co-pays in the emergency rooms are considered to be higher compared to regular hospital visits. But if your health condition is critical, it will be wise to seek urgent care at an emergency room. Keep in mind that the co-pay is sometimes as much as five times higher than when you see your primary care physician.

On the other hand, if your medical condition is relatively minor, you can wait until you see your doctor during normal office hours. This saves your money as well as time waiting in the ER for more critical patients to be seen.

Register yourself in your employer's flexible spending plan.

A Flexible Spending Account (also known as a flexible spending arrangement) is a special account you put money into that you use to pay for certain out-of-pocket health care costs. You don't pay taxes on this money. This means you'll save an amount equal to the taxes you would have paid on the money you set aside.

Although you cannot use your FSA to pay health insurance premiums, you can use this account to pay all qualified medical expenses not covered by your health insurance. Along with paying insurance deductibles and co-pays, you can use your FSA for other medical expenses.

You should note that with the medical flexible spending account, if you don't use the money, you can end up losing it and any amount left in your account is transferred to your employer.

LEGAL PROTECTION

ISSUES WITH LEGAL PROTECTION

There are many legal protection laws for the average consumer in U.S. Know your rights and stay aware of all privileges you have as a consumer. Did you know that there are seven divisions of the Bureau of Consumer Protection?

The **Bureau of Consumer Protection** in the U.S. provides assistance to stop fraudulent, deceptive and unfair business practices. This bureau collects complaints and conducts investigations on people and companies who break the law. It also develops rules for maintaining fair marketplaces and educates businesses and consumers about their responsibilities and rights. There are certain legal problems faced by people in consumer protection laws.

Some of the legal issues faced by these people are:

The **Federal Trade Commission** (FTC) is an independent agency of the government established in 1914 by the Federal Trade Commission Act. Its major concern is promoting consumer protection and preventing different types of anti-competitive business practices.

Every consumer should be aware of his/her basic rights. Safety, the right to be informed, and the right to choose. If any product bought by a consumer causes safety hazards in spite of the fact that it is used according to instructions, the consumer can file a lawsuit.

In case of a serious injury or accident caused by the use of a product, the medical expenses are far more than the company covers.

Consumer Deception is another serious problem. In this case there can be a misrepresentation, omission, or a practice which misleads the consumer. There are certain companies who make false promises that cheat people out of their hard-earned money.

When a consumer falls victim to fraud by purchasing a product or a service that does not measure up to the seller's promises, the consumer may suffer a loss equal to the amount paid, and perhaps some incidental expenses as well. But in all likelihood, the loss to the consumer will represent only a fraction of the amount of money it would take to bring a lawsuit against the seller. In such cases consumers have the option to file a complaint with federal or state authorities in an attempt to have sanctions brought against a fraudulent company, but this will not help consumers get their money back.

Unfair Practices are faced by consumers. Courts have identified three main factors that must be considered in consumer unfairness cases:

- Whether the practice injures consumers
- Whether the practice violates an established public policy
- Whether the practice is unethical or unscrupulous

Economic imbalance is just one the many problems faced by consumers. There are many other issues. There can be serious consequences for the consumer if there is a genuine misunderstanding on the part of the consumer or if the consumer does not have valid proof of purchase of the product which was later found to be defective.

In these cases there may be no legal basis to file a complaint. Lack of evidence might cause issues which affect the outcome of the lawsuit.

LIFE INSURANCE

WHY AREN'T PEOPLE COVERED?

No one knows what the future holds, which is why it is so important to have something that will make tomorrow more bearable, if not for you, for the people you love. With life insurance, you have the promise of financial security. Many people are skeptics when it comes to life insurance, in spite of the obvious benefits that their family and loves ones will reap.

The costs involved: This is one of the main reasons why life insurance is not popular for many people. Given the current economic condition and financial instability of many individuals, it is easy to understand why most people cannot afford to set money aside for life insurance. Besides, the premiums can really be expensive for those who are still living week to week.

Financial illiteracy: This is another thing that makes insurance unpopular. There are many people who do not know the risks involved by not having life insurance. Sometimes, even if the risks are known, people often believe that nothing will happen to them.

Confusion: Some people are confused about the ins and outs of life insurance. This is linked to financial illiteracy mentioned earlier in this section. This is why insurance agents find it hard to explain the risks involved in not getting life insurance to prospective clients.

YOLO: "You only live once" is a sentiment many people live by, however living in the present can sometimes cause a person not to plan for the future. If they have money today, they'd rather spend it on something that can deliver immediate returns rather than on something that will yield future returns. The reality is this method of rationalizing can be very costly down the road.

And even though the internet is filled with articles that tackle life insurance, there are many who veer away from reading or researching the topic because they think of it as a complicated topic.

Given the things that have been mentioned in this section, it is understandable why so many are not willing to invest in life insurance. But if you ask me, I believe that everyone should have life insurance. It's the best way to handle the future in a responsible way. You can sleep with the confidence that you and your loved ones will be covered financially no matter happens in the days to come as long because you have life insurance.

PROS AND CONS OF LIFE INSURANCE

All of us have considered having a life insurance at some point in our life. After all what is more valuable than your life? But as necessary as life insurance is, there are a few horror stories. People have had positive and negative experiences when dealing with life insurance agents.

Pros

The first and foremost reason why people choose life insurance is because of the financial security for them and for the ones they love. It is a horrible idea to leave your loved ones without anything once you are gone but setting aside money to keep a life insurance policy current gives you some assurance that they will be well cared for.

Most life insurance policies include a clause where the insured person can adjust the premium according to his or her requirements. The sum can be increased or decreased, beneficiaries can be changed, and if the policy allows, it is can also be cancelled altogether.

Unlike other investment opportunities, life insurance policies offer risk-free or low-risk investment opportunities.

Cons

Senior citizens might think they (or their spouse) have been paying for insurance all along when really they haven't.

People who don't have any family or loved ones that they want to be taken care after they die may not think life insurance necessary.

Those who have a considerable amount of money in monthly expenses may find it difficult to squeeze out more money for a life insurance policy every month.

For those who don't do a thorough review of your life insurance policy, there may be clauses that you may not understand, which could lead to believe that your policy covers more (or less) than it really does.

A lot of single people think say "I don't need life insurance!" without ever thinking about it. But life insurance covers more than just 'in the event of your death." It is also a way of insuring yourself if you become temporarily or permanently disabled unable to work.

For families whose sole supporters don't have life insurance, their loss can be devastating – both emotionally and financially – for many years.

What are the clauses?

Life insurance normally covers you for a pre-determined amount depending on death, illness or disability.

When death is the reason for making the claim, a lump sum of money is paid out to the beneficiaries to help cover things like future funeral expenses, education, a mortgage, groceries, utilities, and any other day to day expenses for your family.

Illness and disability are handled a little differently. You can choose to be paid in a lump sum, annually, quarterly, monthly or weekly to help cover your medical and day to day expenses.

Is it expensive?

It is safe to say that a young, fit, non-smoking office worker is going to have a substantially lower premium for life insurance than a 45-year-old smoker who works in a factory will. This is because insurance companies factor lifestyle choices into account when making a recommendation on what type of policy (and premium) to recommend to a prospective client. Whether or not your lifestyle puts you at risk for a heart attack, stroke, permanent disability or death from some other disease will determine how high or how low your premium will be.

So think that just because you're young, you'll have a lower premium an older individual. A lot of life insurance agents look at aspects of a person's life outside of their health and fitness. For example, they may review an individual's past traffic offenses. A person who has a history of speeding tickets and other moving violations is more likely to receive a higher premium than someone who doesn't - for the same reason listed above: risk.

Conclusion

Life insurance is more than just 'looking after your family'. It can also benefit protect your ability to provide for yourself and others who are dependent on you in the case of long-term or short-term disability. If your wages go, so do theirs. You see life insurance doesn't just cover your life if you die, but also if you live.

HOW TO CHOOSE A LIFE INSURANCE POLICY

Trying to choose a Life Insurance policy can be a difficult thing. Most people don't want to talk about it, and just thinking about it can make some people sick. Making sure your family is covered in the event of your passing. Having the right type of policy is very important. Some things you should ask yourself are:

- How much insurance do I need?
- What is the difference between *Term Life* and *Whole Life Insurance*?
- Which one is best for me?

Before we look at the two main types of policies, the first thing you need to work out is how much coverage you and your family are going to need.

It's not as difficult as you might think. Generally, 5 to 10 times your annual income is a good place to start. Of course, everyone's situation is different, and taking the time to look over a few things can help you find an amount the policy that matches you (and your families) needs perfectly.

How much do the following items cost your household **per year**?

- Housing, utilities, clothing, transportation, phone, entertainment and food
- Large, one-off expenses like appliances, technology, vehicles
- Earned income for all of the people you live with.
- All insurance policies (property, auto, health, and life)

Once you have a figure for one year, multiply that by 5 to 10 years to determine how much your life insurance policy should be.

Term or Whole life insurance?

Term Life and *Whole Life Insurance* both have their own set of pros and cons. Which one you choose is up to you.

What is the difference between these two policies?

Term Life Insurance covers you for a term between 10 and 30 years. If you die within the term, the policy will be paid out in full. If you live past the term, your policy can be renewed, but most likely, you will have a higher rate to pay. Some policies can be renewed at the same price, but they are normally more expensive to start with.

Whole Life Insurance covers you for your whole life - from the start date of your policy until your death. This type of policy usually has higher premiums. Some plans allow the payments to be placed into a savings account, with a future cash-out option. Premiums are almost always fixed for the life of the policy.

Conclusion

As I stated earlier, there are several different types of life insurance policies, but if you do proper research, take a good look at both *Term Life* and *Whole Life Insurance* policies, make sure you can afford to cover the premiums and that you feel comfortable with the terms you will select for the policy that is most beneficial to you and your family.

ISSUES LIFE INSURANCE COMPANIES

Want to get your life insured? First, understand your tax deductions and death benefits. There is a probability that the first company you go to might not give you life coverage; actually all this depends on their risk assessment models and your financial assets.

Any citizen needs to be fully informed about the insurance company he/she is investing in. There are about 1,200 active companies in U.S. and the industry contributes 26 percent of assets to the GNP (Gross National Product). It is a huge investment field and there are many risks involved, so you need to know what is important other that a flexible premiums and customer satisfaction. There are some basic issues people mostly neglect and they should certainly not do so.

Major problems faced by policy holders:

Taxes: Most policies are not subject to income tax and can be a good tax shelter since nothing is deducted by the state or federal income tax departments. But under certain conditions, like whether or not the policy has stake in stocks and bonds or if the policy taxable and considered a marketplace investment.

So, it is important that you are aware of the tax you will be paying.

Risk management, every company has a different parameter for assessing risk factors. There was a time when HIV/AIDS was assessed as a risk factor in determining whether or not to insure a person. In those cases insurance companies were looking for their own financial security, and not that of their prospective clients. Companies prefer to insure healthy over people suffering from a disease because the risk is lower.

Another risk factor that is considered is the income and assets of the person applying for insurance. Anyone with strong financial background is more likely to get insured.

Many policy holders who become ill or are suffering from serious medical issues have to spend most of their money on medical and living expenses.

If you do not have health insurance, you could select a viatical company instead. Viatical companies are for profit organizations that purchase life insurance policies that insure terminally ill people. Viatical settlement companies benefit the policy seller, who is typically the same person as the insured, by providing immediate cash before the insured dies.

Life Insurance Agents

It is crucial that you are sure you find a good insurance agent. There have been complaints in the past that certain agents will deceive customers into buying new insurance policies which are more expensive just to earn more sales commission. There are not many laws to protect the consumer from such cases.

For additional help and to address your concerns you can always get help from National Association of Insurance Commissioners (NAIC) and The Center for Insurance Policy and Research.

TRAVEL INSURANCE

WHAT IS TRAVEL INSURANCE?

Travel Insurance, commonly known as Roadside Assistance, helps people in cases of automobile emergencies. These companies assist travelers in mechanical issues with their vehicles by providing services like towing, changing a flat tire, jump starting a dead battery, and even providing fuel a traveler runs out of gas.

The history of this service began with phone boxes were placed on major roads at certain intervals, but with the invention of mobile phones an emergency phone network is no longer required.

The first non-profit Roadside Assistance service in the U.S. was started by the American Automobile Association (AAA) provides services to members only, who are registered with them and are liable to some subscription fee. However, these services can also be provided in the form of insurance policy with premiums by some automobile insurance companies. Some car manufacturers also provide basic Roadside Assistance to its customers like towing and minor repairs. The car manufacturers and the insurance companies buy the Roadside Assistance service from a third party. These third parties are usually local towing companies and auto repair shops.

Roadside Assistance Insurance is included in many automotive insurance policies. Generally, these policies provide services like damage estimation, car repair, glass repair, accident damage estimates or stolen car.

Basic Roadside Assistance includes towing, changing a flat tire, battery service, lockouts, and refueling. All these services are just a phone call away. Some popular companies that offer Roadside Assistance are Allstate Motor Club, Good Sam Roadside Assistance, BP Motor Club and many more. They help in all sorts of mechanical failure or breakdown and even if you have a flat tire, stuck in snow, locked out of your car or lost your keys.

One service call ensures help during any emergency. And as far as the annual costs are concerned, you'll make your money back with one or two service calls. In the long run, you will save a lot of money. The most common complaint reported by customers is the occasional delay in service. Almost always this is a result of bad weather, time of day/night, and services calls made on a major holiday.

Some also report issues when they have car trouble in a remote place without any cell phone reception. But that is hardly the fault of the service provider.

BENEFITS OF ROADSIDE ASSISTANCE

Assistance from Mechanics: This is one of the most common used services that Roadside Assistance offers. More often than not, you check your car before embarking on a long trip. However, there are circumstances where regardless of how prepared you are, problems can still arise. There are also times when you simply won't be prepared. But if you have travel insurance, also known as Roadside Assistance, then whether you have a flat tire or a faulty engine, mechanics will be sent to your location.

Towing: If your car breaks down while you are on the road, you may have to have it towed. Roadside Assistance will help you in this scenario as well. There are times when the best thing that can be done is to have your vehicle towed to a professional repair shop.

Medical Services: There may even be an instance where you are driving, and you suddenly feel sick enough to pull over and call for help. With Roadside Assistance, an ambulance or medical team can be dispatched to your location to treat you on site or transport you to the nearest hospital.

No one can forecast exactly what will happen every time you travel. Regardless of how prepared you are, there are some things that are beyond your control. That's why it's important that have Roadside Assistance. With it, you can be more confident as you travel.

TYPES AND COSTS

Some car dealerships sell Roadside Assistance packages with the purchase of a new or used car. Depending on your circumstances, you may need a more specialized policy than the dealership offers.

Below are suggestions to help you decide what type of coverage is best for you.

Types of Roadside Assistance

Two of the most popular providers of roadside assistance are VISA Signature and OnStar. VISA Signature arranges services at set prices, while OnStar monitors your car remotely and communicates with you if you are lost or in an accident. They can even unlock your car for you if you have lost your keys.

What type of coverage do you need?

Try and select a service that will minimize your premiums while giving you maximum coverage. For instance, you can save money on your roadside assistant policy by opting to have the basic towing options (5 miles or $100 coverage) instead of an extended mileage option.

Some other things to consider are:

- What kind of car you own (new or old, American or foreign)?
- Where you live (rural, suburb or inner-city)
- How far you regularly travel (to work, shop, travel, entertainment)
- How often you think you might need to make a service call
- How much can you afford to pay annually for coverage

As you can see, your needs will affect your plan choice prices in a big way.

How much does it cost?

A **Roadside Assistance policy** can cost anywhere from $20 or $30 all the way up to $400 dollars annually, depending on the company, their policy and coverage amounts, and the additional services you request.

Most companies offer different packages with set policies that offer varying types of coverage.

If you choose to be covered by a basic package with 5 miles of included towing but need to be taken further, you could end up paying roughly $3 to $5 per extra mile, depending on the company.

Do I really need a Roadside Assistance policy?

If you feel that you can afford the unexpected costs that come with breaking down in the middle of nowhere or you don't intend to drive too far from your home, chances are a Roadside Assistance policy isn't a necessary investment. But if you do, Roadside Assistance can be a life (and wallet) saver for you.

IDENTITY INSURANCE

DEFINITION

On an average day, you might make any purchase by a check or using your credit card. You may also pay your bills or call home. Most of the time, you do not give a second thought to these transactions, but someone else might. With a very small amount of personal information, someone can steal your identity and use it for their own financial gain. Many insurance companies offer options to cover losses sustained due to identity theft.

Identity Theft

Identity theft is stealing someone's identity, usually their driver license numbers, social security numbers, phone number numbers, IP numbers for a victim's personal computer, bank passwords and pin numbers. Another type of identity theft is gaining access to a person's social media accounts by stealing their user IDs and passwords.

The majority of identity theft in the U.S. involves stolen credit cards. This leads to a financial loss of more than 50 million dollars each year, by the consumer and by the companies who have to refund, remove, and reimburse erroneous charges on a compromised credit card account.

Identity Fraud

Identity fraud is impersonating them and racking up hundreds and thousands of dollars of charges in their name. Both identity theft and identity fraud are federal crimes, and more than half of all Americans have been the victim of it.

Medical Identity Theft

Imagine you have a medical emergency. You are rushed to the hospital unconscious. The doctor examines you and treats you according to your medical history. But what if someone has stolen your identity and used your health insurance for their treatment? In this case you might receive the wrong treatment, which could lead to serious health problems and maybe even death. Medical identity theft is a serious criminal offense, and it needs to be prevented.

PREVENTION

Once your identity has been stolen, you will surely have a big problem. In the U.S. alone, it has been recorded that there are at least 12 million cases of identity theft in 2012. In addition, a trusted research center noted that it takes at least 600 hours in order to restore your identity once it has been compromised. These figures are alarming. Identity theft can be prevented simply by taking care of a few minor details.

Observe caution when shopping online. Online shopping is beneficial in terms of convenience. You never have to leave the comfort of your own home to purchase the things that you need and want. However, there is sometimes danger in online shopping, because of the disclosure personal information, such as your home address and your credit card information. For the best protection, make sure that you shop on websites that provide secure payment channels and have proven to be safe gateways for shopping. Don't be so quick to give in to tempting deals you see online.

Update your passwords regularly. It may be a tiring task to change all your passwords on a regular basis. However, this is one action that will help you keep your online accounts safe. Aside from updating your passwords from time to time, it is also important to choose your passwords wisely. Using your birth date and name as your password should never be done. Make sure that you use something that's hard to figure out. Also don't disclose your passwords to anyone, including those who you have a close relationship with.

Keep your computers updated. Buying and installing anti-virus programs can be expensive. But this is another way to protect yourself from identity theft. This is also helpful when it comes to making your computer less vulnerable to being accessed by hackers.

While the internet has a lot of benefits, with it comes risks, and one of those risks is identity theft. Make sure to be a wise internet user. Do not click on anything without thinking. Do not believe all of the things that you see online, especially if it requires you to reveal sensitive information.

Secure Yourself Opting out of certain services and offers can be helpful, simply reducing your junk mail and limiting how often and where you share your personal and financial information. Securing your postal mail and shredding any paperwork which you no longer need with financial details on it. Some other things like keeping in mind what is in your wallet and installing proper internet security. You can also get help from for-profit services, such as Debix, Identity Guard, LifeLock, Trusted ID etc.

PROTECTION

What can you do? If you are a victim of credit card theft, you can place a fraud alert on your credit report to warn anyone who runs a credit check that you have been a victim of identity theft. One of the best ways to disable someone from opening any new credit under your name is with a security freeze or credit freeze. You can place a freeze at all three major credit bureaus which are: Equifax, Experian, TransUnion. In addition there are certain non-profit organizations which provide identity theft resources and services like the Identity Theft Resource Center and the Privacy Rights Clearing House. Another way is to get some Identity Theft Insurance, which offers to cover you for losses sustained due to identity theft.

If you are a victim of identity theft, it is crucial for your personal and financial future that you take steps to recover. You will have to reestablish your identity and reconstruct any damage caused to your credit score and financial status.

With identity theft protection, you can be confident that your identity is secured and will never be used for anything without your authority.

Identity theft protection covers expenses – generally capped at $2000 – related to contacting credit institutions, legal fees and lost wages, phone bills, notarizing documents, and sending correspondence via certified mail.

Most companies don't offer restoration services or a way to work with customers to help them restore their identities (although this is becoming more commonplace).

Read the fine print carefully

Knowing what your identity theft protection policy covers is the most important thing! While you might be covered for $1 million, what does this mean you will get back? Make sure you look at things like:

- Does the policy help resolve the identity theft or is there only a reimbursement for the costs to repair your identity?
- A deductible is normally written into the clause (generally around $500). If your expenses don't exceed the deductible, you will still be required to pay for the costs yourself.
- Always make sure that you know if you are covered for loss of wages and legal expenses. There's nothing worse than paying the premiums only to find out you aren't covered when you thought you were.

With the small amount these policies cover, there's very little chance you would ever need to be insured for $10,000, let alone $1 million! So, look over your monthly budget and be sure it's really worth it before you sign on the dotted line.

RESTORATION

Recovering from identity theft can be very challenging. The statistics are very staggering. That is why many insurance companies offer Identity Fraud Protection. Certain companies also allow you to add this benefit to your existing coverage. Policy holder who are victims are assigned an advocate counselor to walk them through the identity restoration process.

Counselors

If you or your spouse has been a victim of identity theft, then a specialist will handle the hard work of identity restoration for you and help you to get back to your normal life. Adding identity restoration coverage to an existing policy can make up for some of the expenses you may have incurred after identity theft. Common expenses you may face are lost wages and attorney fees. Talking to an agent about the process of restoring your identity can surely help you.

An identity restoration counselor can serve as a liaison between victims, creditors, and relevant agencies and help in reviewing accounts and making corrections. They may even offer a full year of monitoring your credit to prevent any further loss. If you become a victim of identity theft, a counselor will help you save money, save time and avoid unnecessary aggravation.

Coverage

Some insurers provide employee documented lost wages reimbursement for work time which you lose to meet with law officials, attorneys, and others concerning your identity theft claim.

If you have to reapply for a loan that was denied due identity fraud, the loan application fee is also covered. Costs for notarizing official documents, costs for certified mail to appropriate financial institutions and law enforcement agencies are also covered. Other expenses like long-distance phone calls, travel bills, etc. are included as well.

Minimize the Risk of Identity Theft

In addition to protecting yourself with Identity Fraud Insurance Coverage, you can also minimize your risk of becoming a victim by managing your personal information wisely. You should practice safety tips to help protect you and your family. Do not ever give your personal information in an unsolicited call over the phone.

Be cautious.

Growing Your Business

INTRODUCTION

Business Growth Goals

Growth can be defined as "positive movement over time toward a specific goal." True business growth requires direction and vision. It is paramount to success. Business growth can be measured in many ways. If you set your own terms, be careful not to cheat yourself, speak with your mentor, and set realistic goals.

What do realistic business goals look like? If you have a service business it might be attract the same client for years. While I was driving the bus I was able to service one client for five years, which was a treat. I understood what the client wanted and was able to give him the "white glove treatment" (handling your client's needs with exceptional care and attention). Another client I've been servicing for four years with revenue over 1k per month. While that may not sound like much over four years on your own terms while working a full-time job and going to law school, to many that is truly a feat.

Types of Clients

Noticed I said, "main client." I have many intermittent clients that come and go every three or four months. I call those my "builder clients." I use the income from my builder clients to buy and upgrade technology. Revenue from builder clients assist me in planning my short-term goals. The infrequency of their projects provides a nice pace for me. Since I am aware of what I need to do with my main clients, the builder ones fill up my plate during my off season.

Business growth is not about working every waking minute of the day, but it's always thinking about the next step in your business evolution. I am so intentional about this step that I map out an annual chart of my goals, make copies, and place them throughout my home to keep me on track. I see these goals before I go to bed and revisit them in the morning. Doing this brings me much needed and continual clarity.

YOY (Year-Over-Year) Growth and Revenue Planning

When it comes to revenue, what would you like your first year in business to look like? In the beginning, my goal was simply to pay my monthly cell phone and cable bill. I figured if my business generated enough revenue to those bills I knew I could stay in business. The first month I was able to accomplish this task. The second month I was able to add my car note. Then my rent. That's when I realized I had a viable business. My next step was to "scale" my business (the ability to grow your business without being hindered).

Tools to Grow Your Business

Look for an advisory board made up of professionals who can help you make the best business decisions. Meet other business owners and find out how they make their business grow. Many of us pick people because of their professions, but it's better to find people who have already achieved the goals you have set for yourself.

Lastly, you must allow your idea to grow away from you. If you keep your idea too close, and you don't share the vision with others, then it will die with you.

HOME-BASED BUSINESS

OWNING & OPERATING A HOME-BASED BUSINESS

Life in the 21st century is marked with economic turbulence. Many people are no longer content with a traditional 40-hour work week and have opted instead to seek outside opportunities to increase their earnings. Starting a home-based business is a popular and attractive option to pursue their dream of gaining financial freedom. One of the things that makes it attractive is that there is no need for you to rent a physical space, which constitutes huge savings in terms of operating costs. If you are planning to start a home-based business, there are some practical tips on how you will be able to achieve a high level of success.

One tip that I can personally provide when it comes to owning a home-based business is to make sure that you choose one that you love. If you choose something that you have to force yourself to do, there is a high probability that you won't put your whole heart into it. But once you determine what you are most passionate about, all else will follow. This secret is shared by many successful self-made businessmen.

When it comes to a home-based business, you don't have to start big. You can start small with minimal capital. This is good because it will help you operate within your means. However, if getting your business idea off the ground requires a large amount of capital, you could consider borrowing from a friend or applying for a loan, as long as you keep it at minimum. Once the business prospers and you are able to enjoy a favorable cash flow, you can pay off the loan and consider making more investments that will yield higher returns.

In addition, owning a home-based business requires legal actions that must be satisfied. For instance, there may be a need for you to obtain business licenses and permits necessary for business operations. Also, you may have to hire an accountant to assist you in making sure tax procedures are being followed. Doing it right the first time will spare you from trouble in the future.

Marketing is another important factor in the success owning a home-based business. The lifespan of your business, in part, depends on people knowing about your products and services. There are various mediums that can be used for free while providing you with the guarantee of their effectiveness. Considering that we are living in the age of social media, marketing can be very affordable. More than likely, you will spend more man hours than money.

Home-based business ownership has been proven to be an exciting, exhausting, and daring endeavor, especially for first timers. Keep in mind that the first few steps are usually the hardest. Once things get going, you will become more comfortable, and at times, you may be at ease, but don't expect to sail smoothly to the finish line. Try not to let discouragement settle in along the way. Remember, you can overcome the challenges of owning a home-based business if you remain determined to succeed.

THINGS TO CONSIDER

The decision to work in your home is likely to impact both your personal life and your business. Before venturing into any home-based business, several things should be considered. It's not as simple as it sounds. There are many conflicts – legal and otherwise – that you might experience while working at home. Before investing your time and money, there are some important issues that you need to be aware of.

Establishing a business entity for your new venture. Whether you decide to go with an LLC or a corporation, you need to take this vital step for your business to protect yourself and your company from liability issues. Your tax situation will change when you start your home-based business. New tax laws are passed every year, and you need to stay current on these changes. Ignorance of tax laws is one of the most common problems facing home-based business owners. Also, you might have to get a license for your business, before you actually start earning anything.

Being a business owner and a spouse or parent. You should expect difficulties in juggling the demands of both home and business under one roof. Separating your family life from your business can be straining. A strong sense of self and self-discipline skills will be required.

Setting – and keeping – firm office hours. This might also be difficult. There can be other interruptions while working from home. Certain tasks often require isolation, which can be an issue while working at home. Office space can be another problem. Setting up a home-based business will be less of a problem if your house is big enough to offer extra space for a designated office. On the other hand, limited space will be a concern if you're living in close quarters, such as an apartment with limited square footage. Meeting clients, making good, professional impressions, will definitely be an issue in such cases.

Resources are sometimes limited. The paycheck you take home becomes smaller and smaller, because everything costs money when you are your own boss. Even after "paying yourself," the money you spend on equipment, overhead, travel, entertainment, professional fees and other expenses comes straight out of your bottom line.

There are solutions to these issues. Proper time and space management may make things easier. Hiring a tax advisor might also be helpful. If money is an issue you can opt for free advisors or hire an inexpensive advisor for a short span of time, preferably during the launching phase of your business. This will help you put things in a better perspective.

GROWTH OF HOME-BASED BUSINESSES

According to the U.S. Census Bureau, over half of all U.S. businesses are home-based. It is interesting to note that 70 percent of home-based businesses are successful within three years of founding, compared with only 30 percent of regular businesses.

Many of the businesses began as a part-time hobby. On average, people can expect to have two or three careers during their work life. This is good news for people who have been part of the traditional "Nine-to-Five" workforce and are on the verge of retiring. For them, starting a home-based business is well within their reach. They are ready to work hard and take risks!

Shedding some light on the reasons for the proliferation of such businesses, we can conclude that entrepreneurship in the category of home-based business is not limited to any particular age groups. Nearly 15 to 20% of adults across any age group are entrepreneurs. Some people kick-off their businesses from home and then find a different place to expand, but many continue to run their businesses out of their homes.

Many businesses are consumer-based such as virtual assistants, freelancers which includes numerous subcategories such as copyediting, book writing, and magazine article writing.

Others home-based businesses include accounting, bicycle repairing, boat cleaning services, business plan services, chimney sweeping, cleaning services, computer repair, electronic repairs, event planning, expert witness services, home inspections, household organizers, and various types of coaching services.

In the U.S. most home-based businesses are self-funded or run with the assistance of contributions from family, friends, volunteers and part-time workers. Venture capital contributions are rare. Statistics show that one home-based business in every thousand receive funds for venture start-ups.

Middle- and upper-income earners in the U.S. are able to afford office equipment which enables them to initiate home-based businesses rather easily. Technology and equipment will be addressed in greater detail later in this section.

CHALLENGES TO OVERCOME

There are many people who are entertaining the idea of owning a home-based business. It is an attractive option for more reasons than one. You can start an entrepreneurial endeavor without the need for huge capital. In addition, there is also no need to rent or purchase a brick-and-mortar location because your home will be your office. You'll also save money in since you won't need to pay for employees when you're first starting out. But there are also challenges when you own a home-based business.

Competition: Chances are, you won't be first one with your business idea. With this in mind, you can expect the market to be replete in terms of competitors selling products and services that may be similar to yours. To survive competition, you should find your niche and make sure that whatever you are selling is better than the other choices. Competition is healthy. You just need to know how to deal with it.

Lack of Profit: Owning a home-based business might result in a loss, especially during the first few months of operation. Do not be discouraged when this happens. Even large companies register unfavorable financial performance quarters every once in a while. Instead of being disheartened, focus on how you will recover and yield favorable returns again.

Small Market: As a home-based business, it may look like the market is minimal, perhaps only within your neighborhood. Capturing a large fraction of the market can be challenging. The good news is that it is possible, in spite of the challenges that might come your way.

There are many ways you can promote your products and services, in the absence of having to incur additional costs. For example, online options such as social media platforms and websites, not to mention the power of word of mouth.

It is clear that owning a home-based business is no laughing matter. However, if you are really serious and committed about being successful, you will find ways to get through these obstacles. Make sure that you never lose your passion for what you do. Most importantly continue to invest in your business. By doing so, you will find owning a home-based business very rewarding.

TIPS FOR SUCCESS

There are many people who are interested in owning a home-based business but there is actually only a fraction who have followed through. This is probably because of obstacles mentioned earlier in this section, the most overlooked one being unsure of the nature what type of business to go into. Some prospective owners are also blinded by the capital requirements, when in fact, you can start a business without having a large sum of capital. Even with a little money, you can begin an entrepreneurial endeavor that will yield great results in the future. Below are a few tips on how to succeed with your business idea.

1. **Do not skip marketing.** One common misconception is that marketing is expensive. Another misconception is that marketing is exclusive only to big companies and popular brands. However, in owning a home-based business, you should think about marketing strategies in order to get the word out about the products and the services that you want to offer. As stated earlier, the internet is relatively inexpensive way to market. Just be sure that you are targeting the right audience in order to enjoy a high level of effectiveness.

2. **Build your network.** As part of your marketing skills, you should invest effort and time in strengthening your network. You will benefit from word of mouth that will be spread by family, friends, and other people within your network. It is very effective and the best thing about it is that it's free.

3. **Research your competition.** In owning a home-based business, competitive research is also very important. This means that you should carefully research other players in your landscape, including their strategies and how they are able to captivate a fair share of the market. As you research, look for ways that you can stand out from the rest – this is how you will develop your niche and your marketing strategy.

4. **Choose your business idea wisely.** You might be overwhelmed with how many business ideas you want to pursue. But this doesn't mean you can just settle on any business idea. Rather, make sure to choose one that you are truly passionate about. You should also have in-depth knowledge about the business idea that you are going to choose. This will not only give you confidence in yourself, but your clients will have confidence in you.

5. **Be passionate.** Some people might think that this is a cliché. That may be true, but it is still very effective tip in owning a successful home-based business. With passion, you will be able to succeed. Passion will push you when you're tired, ignite you when you burnt out, and inspire you with new and innovative methods for success.

With the tips previously mentioned in this section, owning and operating a successful home-based business is definitely within your reach.

TECHNICAL OPTIONS

WORKING FROM HOME VS A HOME-BASED BUSINESS

Many people feel that owning a homebased business means they'll be working from home. While the two may share some of the same characteristics, the truth is *you have to leave your home to grow your business*. Working from home is a different situation. I will attempt to explain you the pros and cons of both.

A friend of mine once told me, "*You won't make millions lying in bed all day.*" I truly agree with her. Lying around doesn't get the job done. When I started my business, I'd get dressed like I was going to work and go to the nearest coffee shop. Leaving the house allowed a few things to happen. First, I didn't get that lonely feeling that I was working by myself. Second, once I started going to places where I could be productive, like Starbucks, I found that many likeminded entrepreneurs followed the same routine. And since Starbucks was open, I had a mobile office. I also found another nice place to work from in the morning, full of senior citizens: McDonalds.

Sometimes I'd start the day at Starbucks and end it at Panera Bread (or Cosi's). Going outside of the house worked for me in the beginning. I was able to invite clients to coffee or lunch meetings and still keep productivity high. I liked going out every day. It was a great way to meet new people.

One of my mentors always says, "*Everything you want comes from a stranger. You have to learn how to speak to people to get them to purchase your product and services and you can't always do that from home. Plus, you need to maintain a healthy balance between work and home life.*"

The hard part about working from home is all the distractions. I live alone but I still had tons of them – from wanting to do the dishes, wash the clothes, or clean the refrigerator. In the past I've been known to sabotage myself, so I knew right away I was suffering from avoidance. To help combat this, I started working in the backyard on nice days. I would make my favorite drink and schedule breaks throughout my workday. The gaps allowed time for chores. The best thing about this model is that by working later into the evenings I realized that's when I'm most productive. I am an early afternoon late night type of guy and I usually work my hardest at night.

Working from home requires having the right type of location to maximize performance. Many people work from their kitchen table. I am not a fan of this method. While space may be limited, finding a corner shouldn't be that hard to do. If corners are all you have, consider purchasing a corner desk. Having a desk allows you to leave the space when you're finished working. It also allows you to disconnect from work psychologically. Having a desk shows control; it shows that you mean business. Your desk is your tool.

The IRS defines a home office as a space designed only for business purposes. If the IRS wanted to audit your home office, what would they find? Having a defined area helps maintain the legitimacy of your homebased business.

Disconnecting from work can become problematic if you sit at the kitchen table or on the couch to complete your job. Find a corner in your home, and remember, the corner may have to be in your bedroom. Connecting your work to a defined area helps you mentally shock your system remaining at your desk until what needs to be completed is actually completed.

It's okay to be frugal, but in some areas you can't be cheap. These areas need attention because they could result in the breakdown of your business.

CHOOSING AN INTERNET SERVIE PROVIDER (ISP)

When choosing an internet service provider, make sure that your internet service doesn't just have the best download speeds, but the fastest upload speeds as well. If you are video conferencing, you don't want your picture to freeze. To save money, think about purchasing the equipment that you need. The upfront cost may seem high, but you could save hundreds of dollars over a five-year period. Also, review the industry standards for technology regarding your profession. Some jobs require you to plug directly into the ISP. In other words, Wi-Fi is not allowed.

MOBILE ISP's

Mobile internet service is the next issue to tackle. I once remembered trying out a new cell phone provider. I had a meeting in a major city, less than an hour away. No reason why the service wouldn't work, right? Wrong. The service should have worked, but it didn't. So, there I was, sitting with a client unable to download my presentation. Immediately following that failed attempt, I switch from that service provider and went to another. When it comes to owning and operating a business, sometimes the cheapest deals aren't always the best deals. While you may not need a premiere business account, it's sometimes best to avoid the value plans.

ISP SECURITY

Mobile security is another part of building up the technical side of your business. And if you call yourself a business owner, you should not be using public Wi-Fi. Instead, you may need to invest in a portable hot spot or a laptop that has 5G coverage. My go-to unit is the *Surface Go with LTE*. Having good mobile internet service while on the road is essential when dealing with client's personal information.

EQUIPMENT

Let's talk about equipment for your home-based business. This is another area where people tend to skimp. Your computer should be "future proof" by at least two years. When buying something, make sure that it's up to date for your business standards. Ask around and find out what your clients and your industry counterparts are using. Then go two years ahead. You may choose to have a laptop with an external monitor. Ensure that you back up your work; there is nothing like losing essential data – especially that of a client. Data loss hurts your credibility more than you know.

Picking an excellent cell phone is another important step in setting up your equipment. Don't go cheap. I hear people saying, "*I just need a phone to make calls.*" But when you own a home-based business, your calls are how you make revenue, and you can't do that pinching pennies with equipment.

Make sure whatever cell phone you do get comes with a good Notes App. Make sure that the phone can record calls. Sometimes you need to save the information until you get back to your office. Once again, make sure your cell phone is "future proof."

Printer

Using a standard printer for a home-based business just won't cut it. You need an all-in-one wireless printer designed to help you print, scan, copy and fax like a pro. Make sure you get a printer that has excellent quality. Review all pertinent information on the unit to make sure it's compatible with all of your other devices.

EDUCATION & EXPERIENCE

THE ROAD TO SUCCESS

Many people don't believe a college education is required to be successful. For the most part, I agree with that statement. But I would add that when it comes to operating a home-based business, some education is required. Even fast-food chains have manuals that educate their employees on how to cook, how to operate equipment, and how to provide customer service.

Good business is a balance of education and experience. Both require time and patience. Learning can be difficult but not impossible. Remaining focused on your desired outcome will make the journey a pleasant one.

Understanding what type of learner you are will also help. Some people prefer books and lectures; other learn hands-on. But imagine you had a book on driving a car. You may learn all what all the buttons and switches are for, but does that give you a feel for the vehicle? Reading the manual can teach you the road signs and safety issues – all very important – but you won't know if you can drive until you get behind the wheel. In the same manner, you need a balance of both education and experience to be successful in business.

Study patterns are crucial to success in education and business. You must be able to balance when, where, and how you study.

In this fast-paced world, some find it hard to sit still for extended periods of time and that can make studying hard, especially as we become more digitally minded. Striking a balance between study time and all of your other obligations can make you scream. I tell myself that spending time alone to get my assignments complete is honoring my mind and body, that I'm keeping the commitment I made to myself, my stakeholders and my customers. Mastering time management skills makes all the difference in the world.

TYPES OF FORMAL EDUCATION

Let's examine the two major categories of formal education. The first is college/university and the second is career school.

College/University

Colleges are often smaller institutions that emphasize undergraduate education in a broad range of academic areas while universities are typically larger institutions that offer a variety of both undergraduate and graduate degree programs.

College can be a challenging endeavor when it comes to time and cost. Even though there are many colleges that offer low-cost tuition and many others with accelerated degree programs, some people just aren't in a position to pay for formal education at the college level. Demanding curriculums can be another deterrent from formal schooling.

Many high school graduates are simply not ready for a college level workload, and many lack the time management and study skills it takes to keep up with the pace, much less succeed.

Career Schools

Alternately, a career school (also referred to as a technical, trade or vocational school) refers to either a secondary or a post-secondary education designed to provide vocational education or technical skills required to complete the tasks of a particular and specific job — often at significantly less debt than a college/university.

Career Schools, or Trade Schools, have their advantages. Lower costs, reduced class size, less time to complete courses. Also, you are able to learn skills that are directly related to your desired profession. The cost of attendance is lower.

In addition, most programs that trade schools offer are in high demand in the work force. The only drawback is that most times your credits may not be transferable to traditional colleges or universities.

Most people pick a major based on the expectations of others, namely their parents or guardians. Others chose based what society identifies are the highest paying jobs. Some are led by their talents, what they're passionate about, that thing they always wanted to do.

Growing up, I wanted to be a singer, even though I couldn't hold a tune in a bucket if my life depended upon it. But when I was a child, you couldn't tell me that. I sang all over the house, draining the batteries of my "Walkman" almost every day.

But when it comes to education, I have been able to parlay many of my law student habits into skills to make me an even better business owner. Skills such as advocacy, communication, discipline, organization, time management, and research. Not to mention being resilient and not cracking under pressure.

TYPES OF LEARNING PROGRAMS

Once you decide on a College, University, or Trade School, the next decision to make is the type of learning program you want.

The three types of learning programs are in-person learning, distance learning, and virtual learning. They all have their pros and cons. Over the course of my academic journey I've been all three, and I don't favor one over the other.

For some people, it depends on family dynamics; others like to work late, after everyone has gone to bed. Then there are the people who need to travel out of the home to avoid distractions.

In-person learning is when you learn in a traditional, familiar, face-to-face classroom setting.

Virtual learning (also called e-learning or online learning) uses web-based tools and platforms which allow teachers to simply post resources and assignments online for students to navigate and complete independently. You are solely responsible for completing the coursework individually.

Distance learning (also called remote learning) is a method of study where teachers and students do not meet in a classroom, but classes are conducted via the internet, correspondence, or email. Distance learning is my favorite. Your curriculum is sent to you via email or USPS. You are responsible for reading the material, watching the lectures, completing the work, and sending it back. This works well for busy individuals transitioning to business ownership. I was able to complete an undergrad degree this way. This can be the most affordable way to earn a degree and not miss time away from home and business.

EXPERIENCE

Experience is also gained by being mentored. I hold mentoring near to my heart. It is the fastest way to capitalize on another person's knowledge. But I don't believe in free mentoring – I believe mentoring should be give and take. Paying your mentor is an excellent idea. You're asking someone to stop what they're doing to help you. This allows the mentor to know you're serious about your craft. Cherish your mentor. This person can help push you to the next level.

Being self-educated is also an excellent form of experience but be prepared to pay for it. This is one of the highest costs of learning that exists. While educating yourself is valuable, don't just throw the spaghetti against the wall to see if it sticks. You want a well thought out plan based on your mentors, your education, and your experience.

Real-world experiences can also build character for you. Many students graduate from college without any insight. The lack of working knowledge can be harmful for you. I remember my first management position after college.

At one time I was working for a popular U.S. airline as a checker. I was to check the galleys before takeoff. It was fun working with people from all over the world. There was a management position that opened two weeks after I was hired. In my mind, I had no idea if I was qualified, nor did I even want the damn job.

My supervisor came to me and said, "Everyone else failed the test; why don't you fail it as well." I tried to explain that it wasn't going to be fair; I had just graduated from college. I am a professional test taker. My boss smiled at me and said, "Okay, smart-ass."

I took the test, and when I came to work, everyone was telling me how to negotiate my new salary. I was floored!

Imagine you're hired in an entry-level position and two weeks later you become a regional manager. I was directly responsible for the whole company's operation and I didn't even know what they were.

I was sent to New York and trained. The training was not hard; it was the return home that took its toll—going from the lowest person with the least seniority to the third highest-paid in management.

I cut my teeth and used my leadership abilities to win over colleagues. I stayed in this position for six months. After that, I mastered the career and now I am about to retire.

LEGALIZING YOUR BUSINESS

As the famous quote by the American Entrepreneur - Marie Forleo says, "*Never start a business just to make money, start a business to make a difference.*" Making a profit from your business is without a doubt a good primary goal, but only if the money doubles the business profits at the end of each financial year. It takes an insane amount of passion, consistency, and creativity to start a business that will make both a difference and a profit.

Now let's shift our focus to legalizing your business from an entrepreneur's perspective. First and foremost, be sure to consult your lawyer before springing into action.

BUSINESS LAYOUT POSSIBILITIES

Most of the companies incorporated in the U.S. are either C-Corps and LLCs or S-Corps, LPs, and LLPs. The first two are lions in the jungle compared to the latter three.

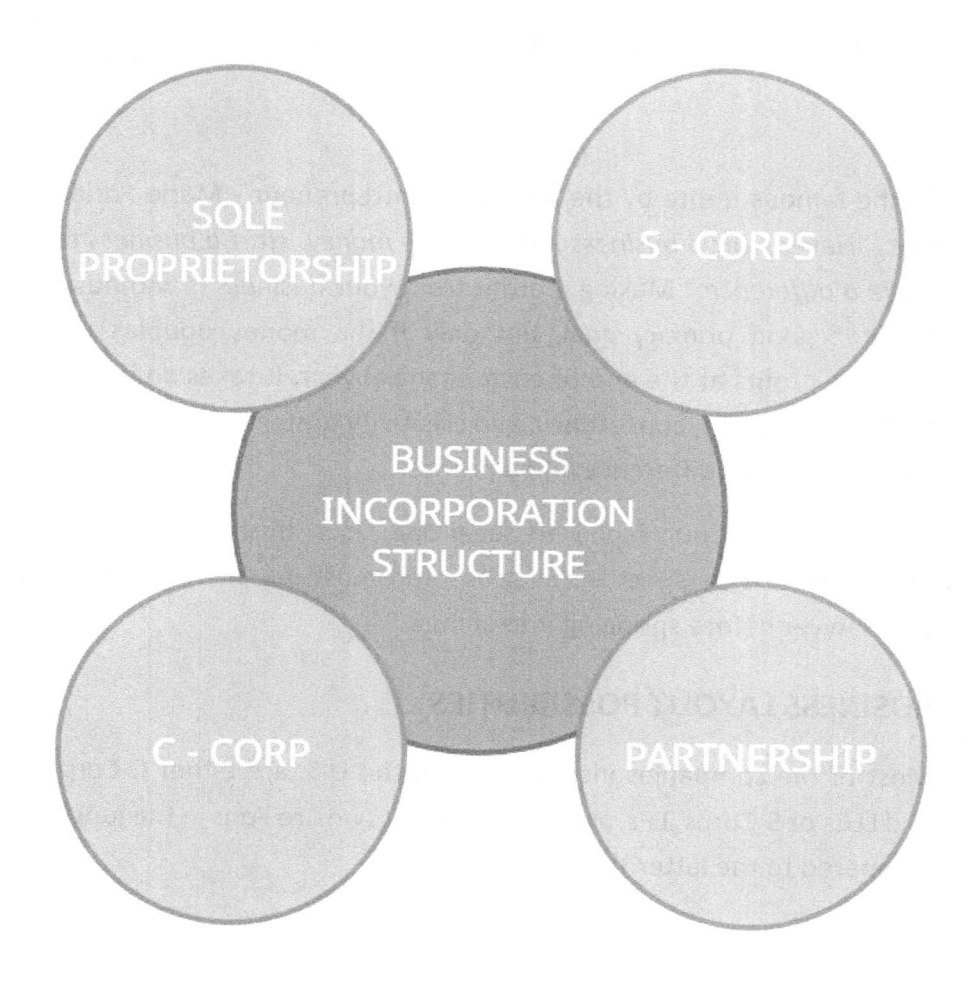

- SOLE PROPRIETORSHIP
- S - CORPS
- BUSINESS INCORPORATION STRUCTURE
- C - CORP
- PARTNERSHIP

The S-Corps and Partnerships:

Selective corporations can register to become an S-Corp (Small Business Corporation) since it requires one class of stock and a minimum of one hundred shareholders having U.S. Citizenship. Besides that, the business firm must qualify to have been an LLC or a C-Corp (Limited liability company or Small Business Corporation).

The C corporation is the standard (or default) corporation under IRS rules. The S corporation is a corporation that has elected a special tax status with the IRS and therefore has some tax advantages. Both business structures get their names from the parts of the Internal Revenue Code that they are taxed under.

Despite the benefits of having self-employment and health insurance tax savings, it is possible to have retirement planning, provided the incorporation meets the required criteria throughout the financial year.

Choosing to get LP or LLP (Limited Partnership/Limited Liability Partnership) is another option. The general partner has unlimited liability for the company's losses and debts, while the limited partner has limited liability protection against company debts and losses

An LLP also provides personal liability protection for all its partners.

The C-Corps:

C-Corps is an entity abstraction layer which acts in between owners and the operators of the business. Taxed by the owners, the C-Corporation companies are the subjects of limited liability, according to the U.S. Federal Income tax law. Shadowed by shares, the corporation gives a portion of the control and ownership to its shareholders, who own upon economic upliftment of the company.

For the record, most of the investors and accelerators usually are fascinated in investing in Delaware C-Corps since it is a profitable way of raising venture capital. Delaware, a state in the U.S. has a governing body of law for the corporations which have accurate predictions in case of legal disputes. Secure right? Another benefit of Delaware C-Corp is that it doesn't require you to make your physical presence in Delaware. This is one reason I made Delaware my home.

LLC - Limited Liability Corporation

Are you looking for personal liability protection in case of business debts? LLCs are a great option since it covers you during in the event of a bankruptcy or any other legal mishap. LLCs do not affect your income irrespective of the profits and losses the company faces. Here's a catch: Members of the LLCs are recognized self-employed, thereby insisting you to pay your self-employment taxations. LLCs are good for medium to high-risk business proposals. They assist you with low tax-rates and protection of personal assets.

MOVING YOUR BUSINESS TO THE U.S.

If you are not a green card holder and you are interested in setting up a business in the US, then an LLC or a C-Corps is your option. Consider this a feather on your cap; you do not need a Visa to incorporate in the U.S. since you could be listed as a passive investor for the company. However, you are required to have a Visa to work for the business while in the U.S.

A widely used business structure for foreigners is an LLC. Yet C-Corps can also be considered according to your comfort. So how do you make an entrance for your business structure?

- Choose the state of incorporation - Delaware, Nevada or Wyoming should be your priority if you are concerned about tax burdens.
- Choose a name for your business .
- Pick an agent who's registered and well qualified in the laws of the state your business will be located.
- Decide the type of management structure for your business.
- Register/File the articles of incorporation with the state, adhering the U.S. Corporation laws.
- Keep all U.S. Immigration Laws in mind.
- Acquire Federal and State Tax ID numbers.
- Open bank accounts for your business.
- Be sure to talk to your tax advisor.

Always consider getting legal advice from the lawyers, certified public accountants, or tax advisors.

Average Incorporation Costs

Normally the Incorporation costs between $500-$800. The state fees range between $650-$800 per year. The compliance cost of accounting and tax filings is yet another expense depending on the state you chose for your business. For the non-green card holders, the fees can add up to at least $1000 each year.

Tax Advantages of Your Business

Legal paperwork helps you protect personal assets and keep your business profits high and your losses low. The tax flexibilities that come with incorporating can add to your savings account, increase shareholder dividends, incurring lower tax-rates, and increase the revenue for your partners.

Now let's talk about a few tax benefits of the business.

- Reduction of Social Security Taxes: Business corporations gives you the freedom of paying only your Social Security taxes from your income and nothing on your business expenses.

- Employee work benefits: Paying your employee when you're not incorporated can be tedious. But when you are incorporated that helps provide insurance benefits for your employees.

- Level-out the loss: You would have the benefit of deferring your taxes when you incorporate.

BOARD OF DIRECTORS

As the name goes, the Board of Directors (BOD) is an elected group of 4 to 30 members representing the shareholders. They are required to meet at regular intervals to manage the direction and success of the company. They are governed according to the bylaws of the company.

The shareholders have a crucial role in the election and removal of BODs. However, Presidential termination due to inefficiency or violations of the company's policies is taken care of by the BODs.

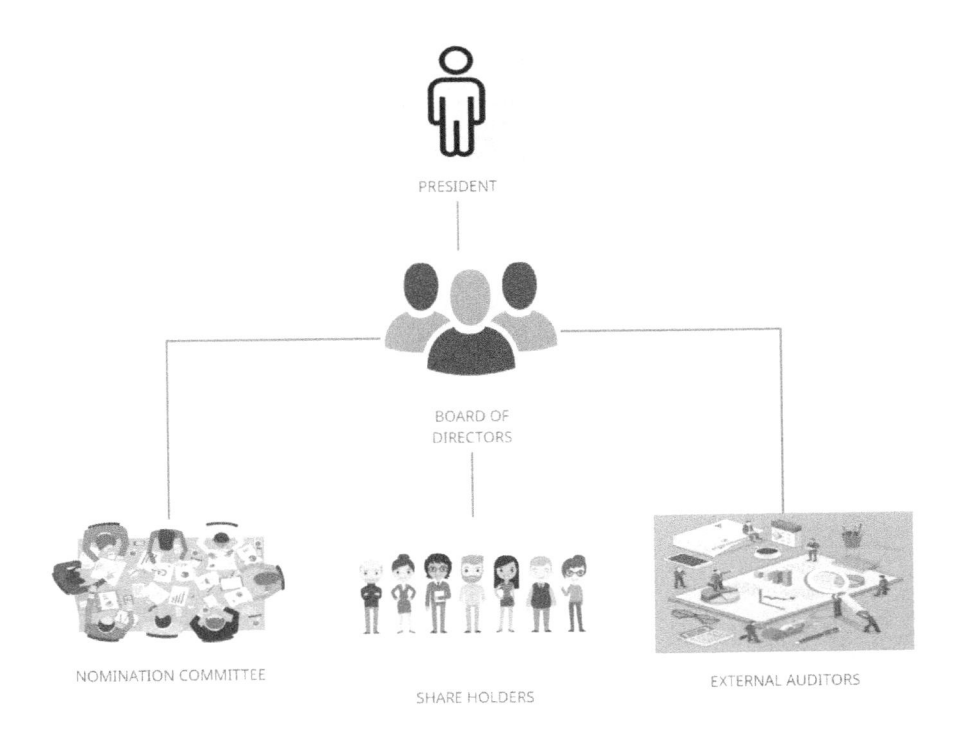

A Call to Action

CHANGE YOUR MINDSET

Why do some people continue working while building their business?

I am in that boat. I have continued to work my full-time career and grow my business on the side. My business is just as important to me as my full-time job. Both positions need my commitment and determination while I try to reach my goals and accomplish my dreams, something that many people are not able to do.

When I first started, I felt guilty about my accomplishments. I had to work through that feeling to maintain my sanity. Building your dreams takes courage and the will to fight, against with fears and for breakthroughs. Breakthroughs that will teach you many life lessons and breakthroughs will teach you good business practices.

Sometimes you may to remain on your "Nine-to-Five" job for your family. Some households not able to make it on one income with one of you in school and the other one working. Other households find a way to make it on one income in an effort to see the business grow. I see this mainly in professional environments. Many of my friends are business or medical professionals. Many partners take turns while one or the other is in training. Learning to respect your home is an important lesson to learn as you grow your home-based business.

Family health insurance is important. Health insurance for yourself, your spouse, and your children is another major reason why people won't leave their current position to pursue business ownership. Health insurance can be expensive for many. But instead, think of your job as a mission to help you achieve your dreams. Now with any mission, there needs to be an end date. Always work with an exit strategy in mind.

There may be a small amount of time needed to build your skills to get the business up and running. Skill building time may take away from your family life. We all have the same number of hours in a day; how we use it is the difference.

I once made a promise to God. I asked that I make money anytime I'm awake, and guess what? The spirit held me to my words. I don't get upset when I need to turn the TV off to get work done. I don't get upset when I can't visit friends because I have a white paper to write. I used to get upset that my friends couldn't travel with me on business trips. I wanted everyone to share in my success. I think heard God say, "Your blessing is just that - *yours*." This became my battle cry, and I live in that truth.

ABOUT THE AUTHOR

Renaldo O. Epps, Ph.D. became a full-time bus driver with the Delaware Department of Transportation on July 31, 1998. While still working full-time, he started his own company on the same date in July of 2007. As the **CEO** of **Dr. Renaldo Epps Consulting Group LLC**, based in Wilmington, DE, he is responsible for the overall development and implementation of Financial Education Services and TurboTax Customer Services. Since then he expanded from Wilmington, DE to New York City, Washington, D.C., and a satellite office in Atlanta, GA.

Renaldo works with Fortune 100 start-ups that have national and global experience. His key areas of expertise include business and educational development, and management with strengths in operational excellence. He has always been a critical communicator and motivational leader with the philosophy of *"Lead by example with the highest ethical standards."*

In June of 2003 Renaldo became an Area Director in his homebased business where he provides individual counseling and crisis intervention in the areas of legal services and financial stability.

Most recently, in 2016 Renaldo became an Independent Sales Associate of Financial Education Systems for which he conducts financial coaching through one-on-one sessions with individuals, couples, and small groups.

That same year, Renaldo also began working for Intuit as a Quality Performance Manager. In this role, he manages over 60 inbound agents, reviewing their KPI's (key performance indicators), and completing his performance evaluations.

In 2019 **Dr. Renaldo Epps Consulting Group LLC** reached a milestone by birthing **24-7 Digital Solutions LLC** to handle all of **Dr. Renaldo Epps Consulting Group LLC's** online customers, as well as the digital components of the business. **Dr. Renaldo Epps Consulting Group LLC** continues to operate marketing services.

Renaldo's educational accomplishments include but are not limited to degrees/certifications/studies from: Trinity Law School (Juris Doctorate Candidate/Expected 2023); Delaware Tech Community College (Paralegal); Penn Foster College (Real Estate, Wills, and Estate Planning for Paralegals); Nehemiah Gateway Program (IRS Tax Preparer); Concordia University Masters Divinity (Counseling); Canterbury Christ Church University Doctoral (Divinity); and John Hopkins University (CoVid-19 Tracer Certification).

From Bus Driver to CEO: A Personal Journey Towards Business Ownership is Renaldo's roadmap for new and upcoming business owners.

Made in the USA
Middletown, DE
09 November 2023